"EXEMPLIFY"

Carrying Vision To The Goal

Dr. Kevin L. Harris Sr.

New Vision Christian Church
9101 Blue Ridge Blvd., Kansas City, MO. 64138
(816) 763-1766
E-mail: Gejesussoon@aol.com

Foreward by Dr. Stacy Spencer

Cover by Dr. Kevin L. Harris Sr.

EXEMPLIFY Carrying Vision To The Goal

Copyright © 2019 by Dr. Kevin L. Harris Sr.

Published by Dr. Kevin L. Harris Sr.

Library of Congress Control Number: 2019902937

ISBN 978-0-9864087-1-7

All rights reserved. No portion of this book may be copied, reproduced or transmitted in any form without prior written permission from the publisher.

Printed by IngramSpark

Printed in the United States of America

DEDICATION

This book is dedicated to my cousin, Howard Brown III. Howard is a fifteen-year old sophomore, who starts the quarterback position at Lincoln High School in Kansas City, Missouri. He actually started at the quarterback position as a freshman in High School which tells you of his ability to effectively play the position. I have watched Howard develop from the day he was born up to his teenage years and I am so very proud of his accomplishments. I am also honored and privileged to serve as his pastor and spiritual mentor. His family nick name is: "fat daddy" and it has been a challenging transition to go from calling him by his nick name to his birth name, but I am finally getting comfortable making that adjustment.

In dedication to Howard, I am donating a portion of the proceeds from this book to his retirement fund. My hope is that he will continue on through college and already possess an economic vehicle where he can continue on through his professional career. Let's go Howard!

I also give honor to Howard's mom Ms. Tomeka Cobbins. Tomeka is a single parent, who has raised her son extremely well and has made sure he has everything he needs. She lives her life for the fulfilment of her son and sees to it that he is effective and impactful in school, society and church. Tomeka is the real MVP and I salute her for supporting and investing her life into the legacy of her child. She has modeled what the true intent of this book is and that is to "Exemplify carrying vision to the goal." Howard is running because of what his mom has handed off to him and I believe he is on his way to greatness!

Then ADONAI answered me; he said,

"Write down the vision

clearly on tablets,

so that even a *runner* can read it.

For the *vision* is meant

for its appointed time;

it speaks of the end,

and it does not lie.

It may take a while,

but wait for it;

it will surely come,

it will not delay.

Habakkuk 2: 2, 3

FOREWARD

By Dr. Stacy Spencer

None of us want to fumble the handoff from God. There is something that the creator has given each of us to do with our time here on earth. Rev. Kevin Harris has done a great job of showing us how a quarterback and a running back are the best example for how we carry out God's vision for our life or our organization.

There is a plan that God has for us that pulls us toward a desired end. We must apprehend that vision and make sure it's not dropped when we hand it off. Not only do our churches or the people lead in other organizations die for lack of vision but also lack of execution of the vision. They fumble it.

This book helps a leader and his or her people understand how to execute the plan so the team wins the game. As Jekalyn Carr sings, "everything attached to me wins!" This book lays out steps for how we are attached to one another to effectively win as a team. Attachment just doesn't happen by osmosis but through intentionality.

Whether you are the quarterback leading a team or a player on the team receiving the ball or vision from the leader this book will help you discover how not to fumble or drop what God has given you. Once you've identified your vision and your position, take a firm grip on what God has given you and execute the handoff. Don't fumble after a hit, learn from your mistakes and get into the end zone to win at life.

INTRODUCTION

This collection of writing is a document designed to inform, equip and empower those learning to play the offensive aspect of football and to understand the correlation between executing offense from a football perspective to also an organizational perspective. There are many similarities between the two and I have attempted to marry them together through a set of principles, even though they are two totally different industries. Football is the most popular sport within the United States viewed by approximately 37% of the American population.

If this many people are watching this sport being played, then there is so much to learn within our society as it relates to the principles of how it's played. I am in no way an expert pertaining to the subject of football, nor the subject of leadership and goal setting. However, I have many years of practical experience both playing the game, leading in Corporate America and leading within the Church setting. I've learned valuable information over the many years of development and have discovered many principles that apply no matter the game, situation or field of interest.

This book is relevant for every type of reader regardless of the football reference. These are principles to becoming successful and winning at whatever goal you have in mind. Allow this book to educate and empower you as you strive toward fulfilling your passion and reaching your goals and objectives for life and business!

What our society need are great leaders. Leaders who fully understand the art of leadership. Our society also need people who are fully capable and competent in fulfilling goals and dreams of those who are willing to take the risk. Whether you are a sports player, administrator, businessman, ministry leader or blue-collar worker, this information will be pertinent and relevant for you or anyone desiring to be successful.

I would encourage you to thoroughly read through this book and take some time to really think about the content you read. Even if it means reading a sentence, phrase or chapter and taking the time to respond to it, by making mental notes or writing out your thoughts in relation to the thoughts you read. I encourage you to read it and perform the necessary actions.

Please, please do not get disinterested or hung up on the football analogy. You may not care for or even watch the football game, but this book is a good way to understand some of how the game is played and more so, the real comparisons to becoming successful in life. I am an avid football fan and I enjoy the analytics of the game and the processes and systems that are exemplified in playing to win.

Read until the end and make your assumption after you have thoroughly read and understood the principles of this book.

TABLE OF CONTENTS

What is Vision, Mission & Values? ....pg. 11-27

Execute The Handoff

Ch. 1	Quarterback / Visionary ....pg. 28-35	
Ch. 2	Receiving The Play (*Vision*) ....pg. 36-40	
Ch. 3	Communicating The Play (*Vision*) ....pg. 41-45	
Ch. 4	Observing The Defense (*Opposition*) ....pg. 46-51	
Ch. 5	Executing The Proper Footwork ....pg. 52-57	
Ch. 6	Placing The Ball (*Tangible Responsibility*) In The Gut of The Runner ....pg. 58-63	

Release Vision To The Runners

Ch. 7	Knowing The Play (*Vision*) ....pg. 64-69	
Ch. 8	Understanding The Timing (*Position*) ....pg. 70-76	
Ch. 9	Proper Placement of Hands To Receive The Ball (*Tangible Responsibility*) ....pg. 77-81	
Ch. 10	Receiving The Ball (*Tangible Responsibility*) In The Gut...pg. 82-87	
Ch. 11	Running To The Right Hole (*When, Where and How to Proceed*) .... pg. 88-93	
Ch. 12	Having Vision To Make Necessary Adjustments...pg. 94-99	
Ch. 13	Running With Authority............................pg. 100-105	
Ch. 14	Gaining Yardage (*Momentum*)......................pg. 106-112	
Ch. 15	Scoring A Touchdown (*Accomplishing The Vision*)...........................pg. 113-119	
Ch. 16	Celebrating The Victory...........................pg. 120-124	
Ch. 17	Putting Your Victory In The Past..................pg. 125-129	

What Is Vision, Mission & Values?

What is Vision? It is the act or power of creative, imagination; mode of seeing and or conceiving; unusual discernment or foresight. Vision is primarily understood to derive from the unseen world or revealed by God. It is certainly an ability to see beyond what can be seen and influence one to make preconceived, decisions a forehand. A Vision is also an overall desired end, goal or objective that one ultimately, seeks to accomplish.

Vision is the focal point in which one is striving and by it, men, women, boys and girls set out to apprehend or directly approach its existence. It is likened unto a person who is at the other end of the building who is yelling your name and is motioning you to them. You see them, but how to quickly and effectively get to them is the only challenge. When there are other people and obstacles between you and the person motioning, it is necessary that you begin to map out or imagine how you can get to them as quick as possible. Vision is constantly, motioning to us in an attempt to get us to approach it.

The Vision is sort of like a magnet that is constantly, pulling you towards it and the closer you get, the more forceful it becomes and you finally realize that it wasn't so much about you seeking it out, but rather it was seeking you out and drawing you towards it.

> **Vision is constantly, yelling at us in an attempt to get us to approach it.**

Visions are revealed and gives us insight on what it is and where it is. And once we get the revelation, it is important that we give birth to what the revelation wants to reveal to us. A vision wants to come forth and it is up to the visionaries to bring it to pass or manifest it within the natural realm of things.

What is Mission? It is the business and routing with which such a group is charged. Any important task or duty that is assigned, allotted, or self-imposed; a sending or being sent for some duty or purpose. Depending on how you define mission can determine how you understand it. In some cases, mission is the identity statement, by which one functions, but I like to look at it as the vehicles that are used in order to reach your vision or overall objective. For instance: If your goal or vision is to attend the Super bowl, the question would be: How will you get there? And here is how you will determine your mission.

I can get there via:
- Airplane
- Car
- Taxi
- Bus
- Transit
- Motorcycle
- etc.

Your mission determines the "how to" or plan of accomplishing or reaching your goal or desired end.

Each will have different time lines due to the capacity of the vehicle and various routes due to the capability of the vehicle. Most of them will have to be linked to the other in order to reach your desired end because of the limitations of each vehicle to function on the roads, highways or airways of operation. Your mission can always be changed, based upon your vision.

Simply put, your Missional vehicles should interconnect with each other. Each vehicle you choose will be limited on how far it may be able to take you, therefore, you must tie them together so that your transition to accomplishing your goals is a much smoother relief to the work efforts of your team. For instance, If the Super Bowl is in Kansas City you would take the plane into town and depending on the distance between where the airport is and the stadium, you would determine the appropriate vehicles you would use in order to get to the stadium. You cannot take another airplane from the airport to the stadium and a motorcycle is probably unlikely. Your best option would probably be a car, shuttle or taxi.

What are Values? They are the governing principles or standards of accountability that your entity, adopts to assure continuity, focus and discipline in utilizing your missional, vehicles to reach your vision or desired end.

Without values, it is extremely difficult to reinforce accountability. Your values are what you agree upon to help you to stick to the game plan and not compromise the integrity of your organization or entity.

Your values serve as the boundaries around your infrastructure in which all are able to move, function and operate. When those values are compromised the group of persons are psychologically, disconnected and the character of the group is jeopardized.

> **Without values, it is extremely difficult to reinforce accountability.**

Values are your non-negotiable principles. They are the things that serve to shape your relationship. A new culture or way of doing things will be birthed out of your value system and they will determine how you interact within your relationship. When those within your group do not adhere to your values, they don't respect the relationship and therefore, hinder or alter the opportunities you have to reach your goals.

When you establish your values, it is also important to specifically determine how you will reinforce your values. In other words, what are the specific things you are going to do in order to validate or implement your values. Since your values are your rules of engagement, it is quite possible to add to them or take away from them as you grow within your organization and you may find that the values of others are worth adding to your team as you grow.

I know there are many models out there, but let's look at the next page and get a tangible, example of what I consider to be: Vision, Mission & Values.

Organization: **New Vision Christian Church (DOC)**

Vision
To become a 24-Hour Ministry in some capacity by providing services to our community on a regular basis.

Mission
24 Hour Prayer Court
24 Hour Counseling & Spiritual Guidance
Outreach
Stewardship Training and Education
Music Ministry to serve: Nursing Homes, Hospitals & etc.
Practical Dramatization's of empowerment
Health & Fitness Training and Education

Values
Commitment – 1. To be punctual at every meeting and or event. 2. Make my service the priority, only second to my immediate family needs and occupation. 3. Develop and maintain a positive attitude, while serving.
Education – 1. Learn something new each month regarding my service. 2. Learn something new regarding my context in which I am serving. 3. Consistency in self-development: News articles, books, training's and etc.
Integrity – 1. Maintain professional relationships with those whom I serve. 2. Keep confidentiality of those whom I serve, except that which is illegal or unethical. 3. Show genuine care and concern for the work and people I serve.
Leadership – Always be a person of positive influence.
Relationships – 1. Meet and Greet people. 2. Serve with a smile and gladness. 3. Stay connected until trust is built.

The Values serve as the boundaries or code of ethics in which keeps the organization in line with utilizing the mission vehicles that will lead them to its vision or goal.

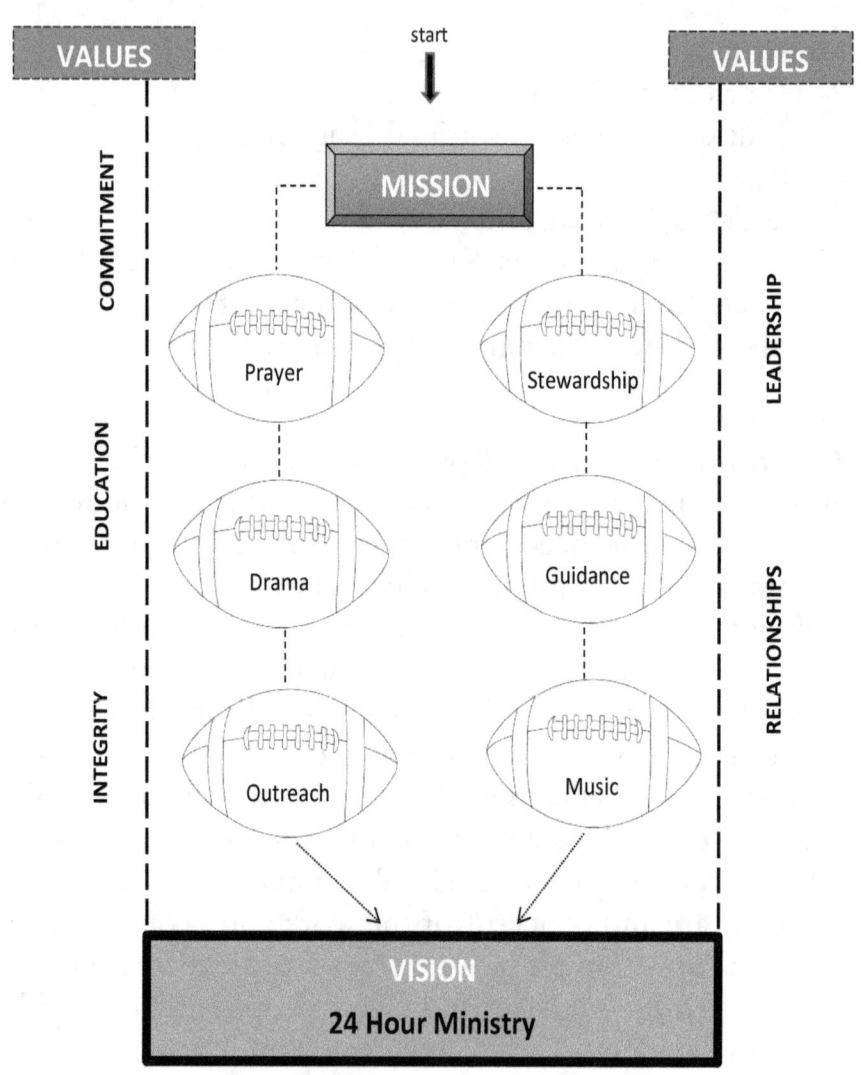

When a person begins to operate outside of your code of ethics or values, then they can possibly lead you somewhere other than where you are trying to go. There will be people who will also bring personal values to the table that will assist them in becoming a more effective servant, example or role model and that's ok, as long as it's not unethical, illegal or immoral. The organization is not limited to their organizational values, but they have identified what principles will guide them into reaching their goals.

What you will have is a system by which anyone who enters in will have a strategic plan to follow that will ultimately, lead them to success! They must adopt your organizational values as their own and not force you into compromising your way of doing things. If their values are good, duplicative and more enhancing than the values you already have laid out, then maybe they can be incorporated within the overall scheme, but you must make sure they will lead you to your desired end. Your goals are achieved within the boundaries of what you value and if they are achieved outside of what you value, it could be a different or illegal obtainment of success and could very well cost you your reputation, good employees, money, service, ministry and so forth and so on.

> **They must adopt your organizational values as their own and not force you into compromising your way of doing things.**

Values are typically developed within a person dating back to when they were young and regardless as to whether they were good or bad experiences, people are shaped by them. Decisions about life are guided by those code of ethics or values that were instilled. Some people can have the same values, but for either good or bad reasons. Therefore, their motivation may differ in how and why it's carried out.

It's not enough to just know what a person's organizational values are, but, why? Why are these your values, should be the question that's asked. Many people never heal from their past experiences because they still carry the pain and agony of what affected them in the past. And because they never share or are taken back to the time they had those experiences, they suppress them and create internal values that they do not compromise.

When someone is trying to figure out "why" a person acts or responds the way they do, it leaves them powerless to often provide what's needed.

> **It's not enough to just know what a person's organizational values are, but, why?**

Every value should typically take you back to a personal experience that was either, positive or negative and it was out of those experiences in which values were created.

Answering the "why" can often lead to a very personal and private place, but if you want someone to respect your values, it will most definitely be important if they understood "why"?

When a person or organization has positive experiences in which they created values, it helps to know "why" so they can repeat those positive reinforcements or not repeat the negative experiences. To share; "why" helps others to know what to do and what not to do. If they value or respect what you value, they will at least know, what positively or negatively affects you. When you can create a culture in which values are shared and expressed, it will also become the standard by which you can hold others accountable.

Without an accountability system within your organization, what are you using to measure the relationship of your team against?

The Vision does exist prior to your presence and you are not trying to reach it, as much as it is trying to reach you. Don't try to pull the vision towards you, but let the vision pull you towards it. That means: as you develop and implement your values and utilize the vehicles of your mission, your vision will evolve out of those practical disciplines and you will reach your destination much sooner than what you may have anticipated.

In a nutshell, here is the focus.

Vision – *What do you See?*

Mission – *How are you going to get there?*

Values – *What disciplines will I need to stay on the path?*

In the game of football, the entire game is played within the field of play. You have sidelines (out of bounds), ten-yard markers (short successes) and end zone (goal line). The overall objective is to get to the end zone. If you don't score, you probably don't win and this constitutes failure to achieve the goal. No organization will last on consistent failure, so it is extremely important to establish good, strong work habits in order to implement them within the game of success. Small successes, equals big success!

Small successes provide constant motivation and encouragement to your team. It creates sparks of courage, willingness, happiness and appreciation while striving to reach higher outcomes. As you continue to achieve, you look up and your goal is right before you! Small things matter and the more you pay attention to detail, the closer you will come to reaching your goals.

Let me talk a little more about values. My values will play the biggest role in my success or failure. I know that a team or organization is measured by its overall success, but even if the team fails, you can still be successful and that is dependent upon your personal values. I will lay out (4) of my very own personal values that allows me to be personally successful.

The ultimate goal is to always pursue team success, but if you lack personal, positive habits it will be difficult to get there anyway and even if the team fails, you can still have some sense of dignity in knowing that you played a big part in reaching your goals. Collectively, your team might have failed, but individually, you succeeded!

My very first personal value is: **commitment**

It will be almost next to impossible for anyone to be successful without commitment. Through commitment I have learned to become focused on what I am trying to achieve. My personal self-sacrifice into the work that must be done is what has brought me much success in my life. No one can invest in you, what you can only invest in yourself and that is your willingness to throw yourself into whatever it is that you are doing with a consciousness of what you are doing, where you are going and when you are trying to reach your desired end.

When I have a good idea of what it's going to take in order to become successful, even when it gets really, really hard I must have the tenacity to keep going and the fortitude to pull from other positive forces and gain the strength that's needed to overcome the obstacles standing in my way. When I am committed, I lay the motivational foundation, necessary for others to become inspired and I set the example of consistency in the midst of un-surety or inconsistency.

> **My personal self-sacrifice into the work that must be done is what has brought me much success in my life.**

When people look at me and my commitment to achieving a goal because of the sacrifices that I make, they understand they will have to make some sacrifices as well and put in just as much effort as I. My commitment becomes the push that forces others to step up and trust within their own strengths because to be a part of something and someone so committed is a psychological revealer of what's in the head and heart of someone who is supposed to be on my team. How can a person look in the mirror and feel good about themselves, knowing that they have not put in the kind of effort that they should have?

My personal commitment is my dedication to achieving success! The level of my commitment will often determine the level of my success, if any at all. Commitment is risky because it can cause you to be out on an island all by yourself. It provokes proactivity and creativity. My commitment to my success doesn't wait for someone to tell me what I need to do. Instructions are very necessary coming from my leader or advice coming from my mentor, but they don't provide me the attitude I should have in order to get going toward my success.

It's when I get going and doing without someone having to keep telling me or holding my hand. That's when I find myself most vulnerable and able to use my creativity to solve problems or provide solutions to potential obstacles. I get up in the morning because God has given me life and breath and I have something that I must get done and failure is not an option. My commitment serves as a taxi for anyone at any time. I am always working towards my goal and whoever wants to help can always find me doing so and I am willing to scoot over and let them help in achieving the goal that has already been identified or in high pursuit of.

> **My commitment to my success doesn't wait for someone to tell me what I need to do.**

Commitment doesn't wait, it initiates! Now let's go for it!

My second personal value is: **observation**

I absolutely, love to observe or just watch what's going on and then discover what can be done. Observation allows you the opportunity to see how things function, operate, process and produce outcomes. It causes you to make mental notes of how and why things connect. Observation, ultimately helps you to make some sense of what is going on and what possibly could be done about it. Instead of always being actively, involved you can be the spectator and enjoy what you see or become frustrated by what you see because you can now see what can be done instead of what's being done, now.

When I'm in observation mode, I just analyze without any preconceived notions or expectations. I study the process from start to finish and see what affects what; when, where and how. Observation teaches me what is, what shall be or what can be. Observation can also provoke vision because the vision is typically the antidote to the problem and by observing, you can discover what to do.

I've also discovered that 'the obvious is not always the truth'. What you think you see is not always the reality of what you see. Sometimes, the surface says one thing, while the underneath or behind the scene, reality reveals something else.

Observation's often answers the question of: *Is what you see outwardly a direct result of what took place inwardly or was there a default, interruption or interference somewhere along the way?*

When I see for myself, I am not influenced by what the public perception is, but I am convinced by my own truth of what I have seen or experienced for myself. Observation slows down the sudden need to make ill-advised attempts to solve major problems. It provides understanding, so when I don't understand why or how, I walk away with a renewed since of discovery and my mind becomes at ease because now I understand.

Just being aware of the circumstances concerning a situation is extremely empowering. Awareness automatically develops a reason for resolve. Most people cannot make decisions because they need a reason to do whatever is asked or needed to be done. However, awareness already gives you the reason or permission to bring about resolve. Slow down and take a good look!

My third personal value is: **creativity**

Aligning your mind with the universe and not allowing your creative mind to be dictated by what you naturally see is a wonderful gift to exercise! Major problems and obstacles have been overcome by the use of creativity.

New solutions, ideas and experiences have been born out of the blank pages of the creative mind and much of our human expeditions are direct results of someone who's operated outside of the box and took risks to be and do something different.

> **Aligning your mind with the universe and not allowing your creative mind to be dictated by what you naturally see is a wonderful gift to exercise!**

When I see a box of tradition or what's always done, I do my best to see if I can exist and reach the same destination, outside of the influence of what has always been. My mind often races with new ideas and new ways to achieve success. Creativity is stimulated tremendously by art, reading, observation and supreme frustration. While frustration may seem odd to you, it is where we develop a strong need for resolve that our minds go into survival mode and begin to become solution based and not just survival based.

There is a big difference between living and surviving. Living is really enjoying the expeditions of life, while surviving is simply maintaining the safeties of what keep us comfortable.

I must live to survive! Life gets very boring when you just live in survival mode. Never taking a risk to do the impossible, limits your creative ability. When you are faced with the harsh reality that it cannot be done, prove to yourself and others that there is always a way. Within the natural laws of opened and closed, there is always an avenue of access to within. Creativity is what gets you in to the thing that was closed and allows you to experience the treasures of what lies within.

When my creative wheels are turning it begins to turn the creative wheels of those around me and we quickly move from being stuck within our problem to opportunistic solutions to our problems.

My last and fourth personal value is: **teamwork**

Collaboration is where you get the most value out of your experience. Being able to positively, influence a group of people is the greatest reward one can achieve. Absolutely, no one can achieve great success all by them self and even if they can achieve with very little support, it's a lonely feeling if you are the only one there to enjoy it. Teamwork is necessary in order to accomplish great success. It is a collaboration of gifts, talents, knowledge, skills, resources and experiences that make a complete package. We learn from each other and gain greater perspective through various inputs and rationalities.

As the old saying goes: 'two heads are better than one' rings true in all facets of life. Teamwork is what puts others on the discovery of finding their own success by tapping into the inner well of personal abilities. A person may never know what they have the ability of doing if they never challenge their mental capacity to confront challenge, change or confrontation.

> **Absolutely, no one can achieve great success all by themselves and even if they can achieve with very little support, it's a lonely feeling if you are the only one there to enjoy it.**

When a team wins, the celebration consists of everyone who is attached or connected to the actual players of a team.

Not only is having a team important, but it's also having the right kind of teammates. You need someone on your team who will focus on unity and calm down the fears within people that challenge their own ability. You need someone who is a heavy thinker, who thinks things through completely and helps you to consider things you may not have ever thought of. You need someone who is daring, risky and not afraid to challenge the status quo or normal way of doing things and you need someone who is very detail oriented and skilled at developing systems of operation and structure to keep you grounded and consistent. My personal values have contributed to the many things I have accomplished in my own life and they still guide me into my future ambitions that are awaiting my arrival. I hope these have helped you enter into your own discovery of your personal values and the impact they can have on you as you launch into accomplishing your own goals and dreams for your life.

Your values are your own personal disciplines that keep you grounded and rooted in self-confidence within yourself. You believe in yourself when you can continue to progress to achievement or accomplishment. You can only control your own personal habits, so be the best you can be for you and the fruit or evidence of your values will be manifested for others to see and experience.

You are your values! I have learned as a leader, your values must be determined and implemented out of your own motivation. No one is responsible for adopting, adhering or maintaining your personal values, but you. A lack of practicing your values can result in missed opportunities or internal chaos. You must drive your personal values forward until your personal values carry you to success! When you are not guided by your values, you can become vulnerable and often times, burglarized of your own sense of self-worth. You feel much better about yourself when you can fully engage yourself. So, now that we have laid the foundation, let's begin our Journey into: ***Exemplify Carrying Vision To The Goal!***

CHAPTER ONE
Quarterback / Visionary

The Quarterback is the captain on the front line of leadership. They could be the Manager, Supervisor, Pastor, Head of Household or etc. He or she is the one who receives the play from the coach to execute out on the field of play. The coach can be the CEO, Holy Spirit, Mentor or etc. He or she has to be skilled on many levels of ability and understanding. Not only must they know what the play is, but they must also know the appropriate line up of the play and their team. They must be able to read the defense and be ready to audible (change) the play if necessary.

Characteristics and skills of a great Quarterback are:
- Vision
- Intelligence
- Mobility
- Physical strength
- Height
- Weight
- Quick Release
- Competitiveness
- Leadership
- Accountability
- Strong work ethic
- Footwork
- Speed, Quickness and Agility
- Good Decision Making
- Patience

Vision - the ability to see and have insight on possibilities and opportunities. Without vision the quarterback will always be reprehensive about ceasing the moments of opportunities.

The Visionary should be looking and observing in order to receive the Vision from God. God provides us with what He wants to do within the existence of a ministry or organization. He already knows what He wants to do, why He wants to do it and the impact it will have on the targeted, context. The Visionary must develop a spiritual eye in order to specifically write down the instructions that he or she receives from Heaven and able to effectively articulate what God desires to his or her team.

Intelligence - the ability to acquire and apply knowledge and skills. If you just jump right in and begin doing, without assessing the situation and applying wisdom to resolve it, you will typically make the wrong assumption.

The Visionary should possess some skills and knowledge in order to authentically and systemically make sound decisions that will in many ways, help the team. If achieving a higher education will help, then he or she should be willing. He or she should not deem it unnecessary to increase the capacity of their skills and knowledge, as well as a close connection with God and the instruction manual that's been given to us.

Mobility – the ability to move or be moved freely and easily.

The Visionary must be ready to move quickly when the opportunity arrives and he or she must be submissive and sensitive to The Holy Spirit and follow its leading, when prompted.

Physical Strength – the ability to exert force on physical objects; using muscles. Increasing physical strength is the goal of strength training.

The Visionary must truly strive to be in good physical health, however, his or her strength is not so dependent upon the physical, but the spiritual and mental. He or she must exercise their faith through confidence in God's Word and prophetically, verbalize and activate their faith as God reveals the plan.

Height – the measurement from head to foot; a high place or area.

The Visionary must have a communication that reaches to the Heavens and they must often, not be found standing, but bending, on their knees or prostrate in humble adoration.

Weight – a body's relative mass or the quantity of matter contained by it.

The Visionary must not be weighed down with doubt, fears and sin in their life, but must be free to function within the favor of; especially, if goals and dreams are to be fulfilled, God's Way.

Quick Release – the action or manner of throwing the ball at a rapid pace.

The Visionary must deliver through articulation the vision to the appropriate person/s within a small window of opportunity. He or she must know how to condense the vision down to few words, without confusing his or her team with flattery and overwhelming verbiage, incomprehensive to the people who are following.

Competitiveness – a strong desire to compete or succeed.

The Visionary must aim for success and not become satisfied with mediocrity.

Leadership – the ability to lead a person, group or organization with great, positive influence.

The Visionary must be able to look behind them and notice someone who is willing to follow them and believe in the abilities they possess.

Accountability – the fact or condition of being responsible.

The Visionary must not make excuses for them self or the organization and crumble when things are not working, but must be willing to take the blame for inferior progress and keep moving.

Strong work ethic – values based on hard work and diligence and a belief in the moral benefit of work and its ability to enhance character.

The Visionary must put in the extra time, effort, energy and resources as their visible contribution to what they are asking from their team and transform the weak or sub par into the strong!

Great footwork – active and skillful footwork within the process of maneuvering; in finesse to avoid the issue.

The Visionary must move with class and dignity; maintain a positive attitude and avoid the traps of the opposition designed to impede the progress of his or her mission.

Speed, Quickness and Agility – the ability to complete a movement within a short period of time with balance, strength and coordination.

The Visionary must accomplish small successes, while maintaining all progressions within the team or organization and coordinate appropriate responsibilities to the right people.

Good Decision Making – the cognitive process of making choices among possible alternatives.

The Visionary must completely analyze decisions through a well thought out process and envision attainable outcomes.

Patience – the capacity to accept or tolerate delay, trouble, or suffering without getting angry or upset.

The Visionary must possess an attitude that is not easily ruffled when challenge or difficulty springs up, but have enough restraint to wait until the entire play materializes and wait for his or her players to get in the right position.

The quarterback actually serves as your coach on the field. It is his or her job to deliver the play to the rest of the team and reinforce who needs to do what, when, where and how. The confidence and encouragement from the quarterback is what motivates and inspires everyone else.

> The confidence and encouragement from the quarterback is what motivates and inspires everyone else.

The quarterback absolutely, must command the huddle and be the one voice that directs the team. He or she cannot be timid and afraid to speak up and direct the other players as to what needs to be done. The quarterback must learn every position within the offense, so that he or she can direct their teammates on what they need to do, where they need to go and what's to be expected.

It almost seems unfair of the amount of work that they must put in, but if the team is going to be successful, the quarterback is the catalyst that makes it all go.

Well, the visionary is the one who serves in the grassroots aspect of the organization. They must have their minds stimulated as well as get their hands dirty while in the midst of carrying out the foundation of the vision. The visionary must influence others on carrying out the vision with proper execution and acceleration. Despite complaints or frustrations from the team, the visionary must command their attention and keep everyone on the same page and moving in the same direction.

The visionary should know how each team or responsibility must function and know how each aspect, ties into the other. That way, when decisions are made, they can be made in conjunction with other decisions that are streamlined within the process. Everything rises and falls with the visionary and he or she must be all in, in order to gain the trust and support from the rest of the team.

As we proceed further into this journey of insight, let us remember that the sight of a visionary is spiritual, as well as physical and their inner eye is just as valuable as their outer eye. What visionaries generally see inwardly is the vision of what they can anticipate to see outwardly. Therefore, they must develop and train their inner eye to clearly see the possibilities that avail them as they physically face unlikely situations and circumstances that seem impossible for them to prevail.

As we discuss the aspects of a quarterback, I cannot give all of the details, however, I can identify some similarities between a visionary and the quarterback. A quarterback provides the details and direction of the play to be executed, while the visionary provides the details of the vision and the direction in which the vision is going and will end up.

The quarterback is on the field of play, providing leadership to his or her teammates. He or she begins with the ball in their hand and it is up to them to either hand the ball off or pass it to an eligible, open receiver. All organizations and or ministries rise and fall depending on appropriate leadership. The visionary receives the vision from God and then he or she writes it down within an organized fashion and then, articulates it to the rest of the team.

The visionary is the catalyst that drives the vision home within the hearts and minds of the team and provides the development and strategies to enhance the opportunity to be successful.

The visionary must dictate the faith of the team and encourage everyone to just believe in what their God has said and trust that if they do their part, He will do His part.

The visionary and the quarterback are different as it relates to whom they receive the vision from. The quarterback receives the play from the coach and it is up to the quarterback to scan the defense and if the defense is positioned to stop the potential play, they have the authority to audible (change) the play at the line of scrimmage.

However, the visionary may or may not have that same authority, depending on who his or her boss may be.

If it is for a secular corporation, then in most cases they have the freedom to alter the play, but if it's under the leadership of God, you have no authority to change what God has instructed, despite the presumed opposition.

Nonetheless, you must believe in your team and their ability to execute. Many challenges may be easier than others and extra efforts may have to be put in more so than others, nonetheless, that's what you all have worked so hard for.

Visionaries are designing the effectiveness of the execution as well as scoping out the opposition that is often in the way of their achievement.

> **Nonetheless, you must believe in your team and their ability to execute.**

The more you can access the defense, the better chance you have for designing a plan for success.

CHAPTER TWO
Receiving The Play (Vision)

There are only few quarterbacks who call their own plays. The one's who do, have a special, unique gift which allows them to be able to run an offense by their own intellect. They are the ones who not only can see their offensive strategy, but also able to read the variations of the defense and call the right play for the right line up. They also have an ability to beat the defense to their spots. As I said at the beginning of this paragraph, only few can call their own plays and are given permission to do so.

Most quarterbacks have to receive their play from either the offensive coordinator, coach or rotating player, who's entering the game. Once a play has ended, the quarterback must begin preparing to receive the next play. He or she cannot spend much time celebrating the success of one play because there is so much more progress to be made and many more plays to be executed.

> **The ones who do, have a special, unique gift which allows them to be able to run an offense by their own intellect.**

There is a time clock that limits the amount of time, between plays and the quarterback must round up his or her team and prepare to give them the next, designed play.

The quarterback has to depend on his or her coach, who are not necessarily on the field of play, but are watching it from a distance or an overview perspective.

There are many things that must be considered and what the quarterback may not be able to see, the coach does see and it is their job to call the appropriate play. You must look intently to the coach or listen intently to the one bringing in the play, so as to not call the wrong play or give misguided instructions. The quarterback must develop some disciplines in order to be ready to receive the play from the coach or rotating player. He or she must thoroughly, study the playbook and know the various signs and hand signals that's used to identify and distinguish, plays. He or she needs to spend much time with the coach and build a collaborative, trustworthy relationship.

The quarterback/visionary must clear his or her head and look intently for the play. Your mind must not be cluttered with other information, past failures and setbacks, uncertainty or nonessential thoughts that draws attention and get in the way. His or her mind should be prayerful, watchful and sensitive to the voice of The Holy Spirit as He speaks the next direction.

Functioning as the quarterback can sometimes become frustrating when you are not clear or when it seems to take too much time to receive the next play, but you must stay calm and confident and do not buckle under pressure. Once the quarterback receives the play, he or she must process within their mind the aspects of the play and articulate it to their team.

If the quarterback does not remember what the play is or what it entails, then they are handicapping the possibilities of progress or success. If they are stumbling trying to communicate the play, the team will be confused as well and it will probably turn out to be a busted (non-progressive) play. If there is too much confusion, the quarterback has a right to call a timeout and get clarification from the coach (visionary). This means you must huddle up (call a brief meeting) and re-articulate the play.

Do not try to execute your play (vision) when there is much confusion. Everything that you do is designed to bring you much closer to your goal, so make sure everyone is clear on what it is that you are implementing or trying to accomplish. If you need to call a "time out" (meeting); do so and don't take for granted that everyone who needs to know, understands and are confident in what they are supposed to do.

> **Do not try to execute your play (vision) when there is much confusion.**

Sometimes people will nod their head or say that they understand, when in actuality they are not clear. Ask them to articulate back to you what it is that they are supposed to be doing. If they can, it just reinforces the fact that they know, but if they can't, it means you may have to express it again or in another way that is less complicated. Confusion is designed to impede the progress toward a common goal. It sometimes; manifest through: frustration, arguments, restraints, untimeliness, miscommunication and possible, dissolution of a team.

You must provide clarity, a plan of action, leadership development, points of wisdom and various means of resources to ensure that everyone is on the same page and that everyone is full steam ahead as it relates to accomplishing the common goal.

Remember, your play is coming in to you from the sideline or upper box. Those from a higher plane or outer perspective are looking at things from a much broader range and they often see things that you do not see. I know you're on the field and you're right in the thick of things, but you must trust your coaches and not override the play they send in or take for granted what they believe is the best play for the current situation.

Quarterback's / visionaries sometimes think that the coach just doesn't understand, doesn't care or is out of touch with what is going on and I am here to tell you, they could be further from the truth. The coach is very much aware and very much in tune and there are other variables that must be considered. From a theological perspective, the visionaries' coach is God, The Holy Spirit is the play and Jesus is the manifestation or result of the play.

When the visionaries' is in harmony with the whole of God, he or she is more susceptible to accomplishing the desired results of the play. You cannot be in conflict with God and expect to receive the play and execute it within an obedient, effective manner.

What you think is best, may not actually be what is best for the overall situation. Do not put your will above God's Will and think that you can call your own shots better than what

He could call them. You are not God and neither do you have any of His Sovereign attributes. God is All-knowing! He knows everything from the beginning to the end, in the midst of where things lie right now. Trust Him! Don't question what He is doing or developing within yourself or your team. Just call the play.

It is always a great practice to verbally pronounce the play once you receive it for self-reassurance, correctness and memorization. This practice helps you to maintain what you've heard and increases your chances of repeating it correctly. Even if you repeat it within the ears of your inner conscience, it allows you to listen and say what it is you heard. You are the quarterback / visionary and it is ok to talk to yourself. You have a great responsibility to repeat what you heard, so make sure you heard it right and don't worry about people's perceptions of you.

As long as you can appropriately, repeat what you heard from God, you will have the advantage over the opposition or enemy you are facing which is designed to stop you from reaching your goal.

As the quarterback or visionary, you have the ability and the authority to speak what the coach or God has said to you and no one can change, alter or discredit what you have been given. So, the question is: Do you believe in what you've heard?

> **Even if you repeat it within the ears of your inner conscience it allows you to listen and say what it is you heard.**

CHAPTER THREE
Communicating The Play (Vision)

The quarterback has to communicate the play to the rest of the team. He or she is generally the only one talking within the huddle. He or she gives the play, snap count and any other instructions to specific players. When the play has been communicated, there is typically a general clap and then braking of the huddle. The clap and brake insinuate that everyone gets it, understands it and is ready to execute it on the playing field.

Communication is the key factor to accomplishing anything, on any level, at any time or place. Whenever it involves more than one, the ability to communicate is vitally essential in order to share information. Every relationship's success is relegated on effective communication or ability to exchange information. If people aren't talking, chances are, their relationship is suffering from the lack of both parties not being on the same page or understanding the strategic plan.

Even if there is no verbal communication, there are other forms to exchanging information like nonverbal expressions such as: Eye contact, sign language, symbolisms, body language, temperament and etc. You have to communicate in order to share important information. When there is no communication you actually begin to work against your teammate because your expectations, challenges, goals and realities are different than that of your teammate and you must connect in order to proceed.

If you don't talk, your relationship will become hampered by assumptions and assumptions can provoke frustration and frustration can lead to alienation and alienation will produce isolation and isolation leads to stagnation.

Who wants to be in a relationship that isn't going anywhere? When you are stagnant, you aren't going anywhere or accomplishing anything that will impact your collaboration. Therefore, your goals will go unfulfilled and your purpose will lose its direction.

> **When you are stagnant, you aren't going anywhere or accomplishing anything that will impact your collaboration.**

The play that has been delivered for you to communicate has already been well thought out and scrutinized, it's now your responsibility to share the play with your teammates.

Communicate in these attributes:

With *Strength*: There must be forethought and strong, vocal articulation.

Once the specific direction has been given to you as the visionary, you must play it through within your mind and visualize it actually happening. Your mindset determines how you view it. Almost no one intentionally, visualizes failure. We see it with much possibility and success and that is the way you must communicate it to your team.

Confidence.: Strong belief and conviction with no hesitation within your voice.

You are actually selling to them what God has shown you and you must make believers out of them in terms of what they see. Learn the characteristics and qualities of a good salesman. As the visionary, you have seen God work before and what may be impossible with human ability, is very possible with supernatural ability! Do you believe in what God has said or shown or do you doubt? I encourage you to first look at the potential. If you cannot see the potential, it will be very hard for you to establish the possibility. Potential is: *having or showing the capacity to become or develop into something in the future.* Possibility is: *the state or fact of being likely or possible; likelihood.* The potential is what sparks the possibility and these two things together become the motivation to pursue your dream/s.

Legibility: Easy to decipher or distinguish what needs to be done.

The vision that you are sharing or communicating should be said in a way that your teammates can hear, understand and confidently respond. You cannot fumble your words or stumble through the explanation of specifics. If you fumble, chances are: your runners will fumble because they did not have the vision secure within their minds and cannot carry out the application. Slow down, state the vision, ask and answer any questions, reinforce what you already said and execute the application.

Clarity: Intelligibly and in particular.

As the visionary you actually are representing God and speaking on His behalf, as you speak as if God, Himself is speaking. Therefore, how you say it should be in the same way He says it. It must be communicated clearly and precise with sensible, articulation.

Not too lofty, where it hovers above the heads of your team and not too vague, where it does not connect with self-starters, who can take the information and run with it. The communication should be engaging, inspiring, somewhat challenging, but achievable. This type of communication is what brings all levels of people together, working towards a common goal.

and *Expectation*: Belief in the affect or outcome.

From your point of view, it's not if it happens, but when it happens. When you can communicate the play in this fashion, your teammates will rise up to the expectation and become confident within their own area of responsibility and desire to do their part.

When you communicate with total belief in the vision, you always provide a next step, after you have given the specific instructions to carry out.

> **From your point of view, it's not:**
> *(if)* **it happens,**
> **but (*when*) it happens.**

This way, you always remain a step ahead and allow yourself to be better prepared for whatever obstacles may come your way.

Providing a next step is the assurance you have within the preceding instructions you have given and thus provide a victorious mentality within the minds of your team. When your eye is on the prize, it psychologically prepares you to overcome the obstacle that's in the way of gaining the prize. Communicating the vision is extremely important to the implementation of who, what, when, where and how, you will accomplish the goal.

Remember, you are speaking for God and your vision is God's vision; revealed to you and if anyone is going to team up with you, you must share with them what God has shown you and it's your job to get them to buy in and adopt the vision for themselves. If they don't take ownership, they probably won't participate. You need as many gifts and skills possible, in order to reach your goal. If you are not excited about what God has shown, you won't communicate it in a way that excites your team.

God has assembled your team, so that He can reveal to you His dream. Your team is not your team, but God's team, He assembled with you. God holds you accountable for communicating the dream and executing the plan, so don't mismanage or take for granted the many people He will send to assist you in accomplishing this dream that you cannot achieve on your own.

If you are the visionary, you are also the mouthpiece! If your team is going to hear what God has said, it must come directly from you. In some way shape, form or fashion, God is always speaking, so what has He said?

CHAPTER FOUR
Observing The Defense (*Opposition*)

Once the quarterback communicates the play and then breaks the huddle. He or she then, observes the position of the defensive players and discerns how the play will be defended. He or she understands that the play should be executed at the weakest point of the defense or where there are gaps or less opposition in stopping or hindering the play.

The quarterback should be able to read the defense and understand that if the play which was called, will continue, will the chances of it succeeding, be hopeful or doubtful? Is there a blitz? Which side or area will the blitz come from?

> **He or she understands that the play should be executed at the weakest point of the defense or where there are gaps or less opposition in stopping or hindering the play.**

Is the defense overloaded to the left, right or middle? How many linebackers are in the middle of the field? How many defensive backs are in the secondary? How many down linemen are there? All of these questions must be observed by the quarterback and answered within his or her own mind within a very small window of time. If he or she is satisfied, he will continue on with the play that was called or he may have to call a timeout, take his chances or change the play at the line of scrimmage.

The visionary should seek to know and understand the easiest obstacles or hurdles to overcome in achieving his or her goal and empower his teammates or supporting cast to rectify the issue as soon as possible.

Well, those same set of questions must be answered by the visionary.

1. **What immediate obstacles do we have that are confronting us?**

    - *For example: If the immediate, goal of the vision is to obtain property*, do we have the money to obtain it?
    - Will our team agree to support the long-term efforts of procuring and maintaining the property?
    - Is the property free and clear of any liens or debts?
    - Do we have a guaranteed lender?

    There are obviously many more initial questions to be answered, but the visionary must observe these things before he or she can move forward.

2. **Do we have individuals with certain skill sets who are a part of our team and willing to help?**

    - Regarding property, do we have real estate agents, accountants, bankers, builders, carpenters, lawyers and etc.? These people are your blockers against the defenders of reaching your goal.
    -

3. **Are most of our challenge's legal issues, property or land issues, financial issues or etc.?**

   - In what priority should I rate my issues? Should I work on an issue one at a time or should I work on several simultaneously?

   - Have I identified the best possible agents to deal with these issues and if needed, do I have the financial resources to compensate them for their service?

Of course, these are not all of the questions that need to be asked, but certainly some to consider.

Observing the defense would also mean that as the quarterback, you would have to understand the role and functionality of each defensive player in order to understand how their assignment can impact your designed, play.

It's not just seeing where they are, but what their intent is to destroy your progress.

Visionaries must know the negative impact each obstacle can have on reaching their goals. They don't sit back and let things happen, they make things happen by being proactive in dealing with issues before they occur.

They have thought out the potential problems and have devised a plan to counter balance or overcome the potential problems.

A visionary's greatest offense is his or her ability to understand the defense and the most effective way to get around the obstacles.

They don't sit back and let things happen, they make things happen by being proactive in dealing with issues before they occur.

Example of Offensive play and Defensive alignment

As the quarterback, let's consider the designed play and observe the aligned defense. The offensive players are represented by circles, while the defensive players are squared. Most of the defense are aligned and overloaded to your right side of where the potential play will run. The quarterback should then observe the defense and change the play at the line of scrimmage.

The <u>bold</u> lines identify the original play and the <u>dotted</u> lines reveal the changed play.

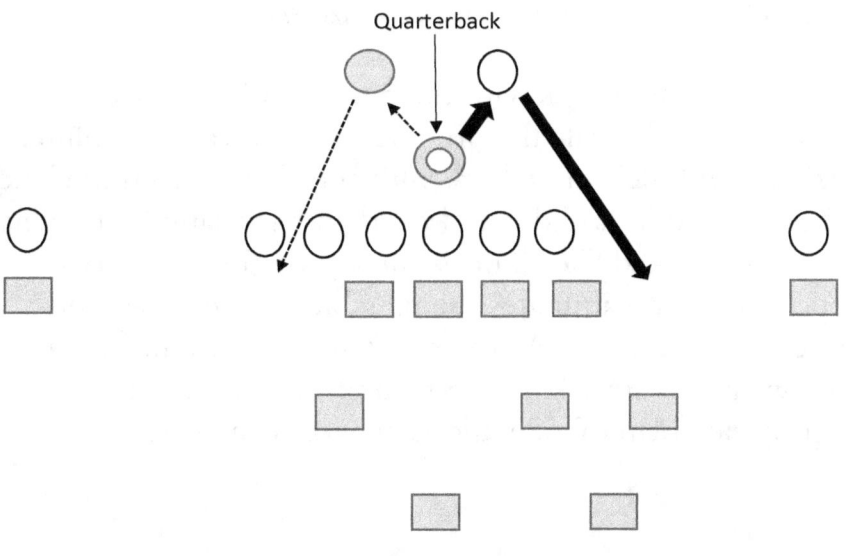

The quarterback will have much more success if he or she change the play to hand the ball off to the (gray) running back because there are lesser defenders on your left side than on your right side. Therefore, the chance of gaining more yards or scoring are greater by switching the play to the left.

If the quarterback continues on with the original play that was called, he or she is subject to gaining no yardage or losing yardage due to the defense having more defenders on that side, waiting to prohibit or stop the progress.

Likewise, the visionary must observe the immediate issues and design an alternate route in reaching the goal. That is a skill set that he or she must learn and develop. The previous characteristics and skills on pages 28-32 will be necessary in order for the visionary to pull this accomplishment off with success. When God instructed twelve officers of Israel to go and spy out the land of Canaan, He sent them to observe, investigate, bring back fruit and visualize themselves obtaining the land. (*Numbers 13*)

When they came back with the report, only two had a positive report, while the other ten saw defeat and failure. Joshua and Caleb came back with actual fruit from the land. They smelled it, tasted it and brought back samples of what it actually looked like. This is the job of the visionary to report to your teammates the tangibles, possibilities and necessary resources. As the visionary, you are the witness that what you are asking can be done and with the appropriate plan of operation, the goal can be achieved!

Observing the opposition or your enemy, helps you to know their strengths and weaknesses. When you know your enemy, it better prepares you on how to attack, where to attack, when to attack and what to attack it with. You gain the upper hand and it allows you not to just sit back and respond to the opposition, but rather attack first and eliminate it's plot or plan to destroy you.

> **The previous characteristics and skills on pages 28-32 will be necessary in order for the visionary to pull this accomplishment off with success.**

Whenever quarterbacks are preparing to face the next team, they study film on their opponent. They spend hours and hours of time studying what they do, their strengths and weaknesses. So is the responsibility of the visionary, to know your opponent and it's tendencies. Not only are you preparing yourself, but also your teammates on how to overcome the enemy.

Observation requires much of your time, attention and planning. Your enemy cannot surprise you when you know the weapons of its warfare. You can determine your success by defeating the oppositions that confront you. They will occur, but the better prepared you are to face them the more they will become a disadvantage to you.

Stop getting paralyzed at the opposition you see. Big success, typically comes with big opposition, so square up, take a deep breath and pursue the goal.

CHAPTER FIVE
Executing The Proper Footwork

Once the ball gets hiked into the hands of the quarterback, it is then his or her job to hand the ball off to the running back. Though it may seem easy and without question, simple to do, one must understand that it takes an amazing amount of footwork to make this happen. The quarterback receives the ball from the center and then he or she must effectively receive the ball, take a step or two backwards, turn to the left or right direction and hand the ball off. The feet must have balance, agility and proper timing.

If the quarterback does not provide proper footwork, the running back may already be at the intended spot, but the quarterback may not be there yet, thus causing a failed or inferior play. If the quarterback's timing is off, it will throw the entire play off and it will make the rest of the team look bad because of the clumsiness, footwork of the quarterback.

The visionary must also provide proper footwork. He or she should possess agility and balance when handing vision off to those who are intended to carry the purpose. While the quarterback is taught to be light on their feet and not weighted down and off balance, the visionary should be free from stress, anger, frustration and resignation, especially as he or she is trying to hand the purpose, goal and responsibility of the vision to someone who's willing to carry it.

There are various, practical ways a visionary can relieve the tension and they are as follows:

1. Take deep breaths, inhaling and exhaling
2. Prayer for inward fulfillment and satisfaction
3. Meditation by closing your eyes and thinking on the strategy of your outcome
4. Five minutes of exercise (arms, neck, shoulders, leg lifts or a simple walk)
5. Receiving periodical body massages to tense areas

There are certainly more things that can be done to relieve the tension. However, if your mind or thoughts aren't collected, you will hand off to your runners the same disconnected energy that you have and what frustrates and anger's you will frustrate and anger them. It will soon cause them to give it back to you rather than use their ability, creativity and innovation to reach the goal or objective.

The visionary must possess a balance within his or her implementation or delegation of responsibility. One form of balance means: an equal share of workload. When you overload one aspect of your team, without giving an equal share to others, it can easily become overwhelming to those who are doing most of or all of the work, just as the quarterback cannot put more weight on the leg, which is on the same side as the runner.

If the quarterback does put more weight on the leg on the same side as the runner, it can cause him to lean forward and stumble or bump into the running back or the one he's

> **If your mind or thoughts aren't collected, you will hand off to your runners the same disconnected energy that you have and what frustrates and anger's you will frustrate and anger them.**

handing the ball off to. This means that you disrupt the timing and progress of the runner and could cause you to lose yardage or progress. Bad footwork is one of the reasons why ministries or organizations work against each other. Agility, timing and balance are all necessary to the effectiveness of getting the vision out from the office or interior leadership, into the outer walls and exterior of your supporting cast. The vision is not meant to stay between the visionary and the frontline leadership, but out to the rest of the team and into the area in which you are called to serve, obtain and fulfill.

If the visionary cannot show signs and abilities of running, it's going to be very difficult for the rest of the team to support his or her efforts. When the visionary is all in, the rest of the team feeds off of his or her energy and makes the level of sacrifice bearable because the visionary has made various aspects of sacrifice, them self. The visionary cannot be too slow or too fast, but must work on the perfect timing of handing the vision off to the running supporters. When your timing is off, you could very well miss the opportunities that are awaiting your arrival.

When God speaks or when intuition says: now's the time to do this or to do that, don't wait or second guess what needs to be said or done. Timing is everything! The quarterback must be in the right spot, at the right time in order to hand the ball off. If the runner is late, it reveals their struggle, mishap or weakness, but it also forces them to pick up the pace and perfect their timing.

> **When your timing is off, you could very well miss the opportunities that are awaiting your arrival.**

The quarterback makes the running back adjust to his or her timing. Time is passing by and you can never regain it back, so you must take full advantage of the time you are allotted now or it will ease by and pay no attention to your presence. You have to attract attention by being at the right place at the right time.

Most genuine supporters aren't lazy, they're just waiting on the visionary to hand the vision off. Visionary's slow people down who are willing and ready to do their part, but because of slow, doubtful, insecure visionaries, the goals are not being reached and obtained and yet the visionary is complaining about having to do it all by themselves.

When the visionary can identify someone, who is willing and ready to carry a part of the vision, he or she should take the opportunity and sit down with that person and discuss their gifts, skills and abilities. Sometimes the visionary waits too late to do it and their motivation becomes hindered by the lack of concern or complaints by others and suddenly, they lose the energy to do, embrace or encourage the thing that you desire. In other words, they become discouraged by the attitudes and lack of concern by others and feel like they will be fighting an uphill battle.
Don't allow disconnected people to disease your highly motivated people by allowing them to drain them of their desire and inspiration.

As the visionary, you must meet with these people and keep their motivation up and deposit your energy into their energy and raise the level of the overall, inspiration to a much higher level. Your self-development will either help or hinder their self-development. If you are ever working, learning and increasing, they will likely follow your lead.

Learn how and when to pick up the pace or slow the pace down. Don't let a highly motivated person determine what the vision is going to be, that's your job as the visionary. In cases like this, you have to slow them down and help them to reconnect to the vision that has already been given.

> **Don't let a highly motivated person determine what the vision is going to be, that's your job as the visionary.**

The task of dealing with highly motivated people is that sometimes they have their own agenda's and when they simply cannot do it themselves, they come into an already established infrastructure and attempt to use that support system to accomplish their agenda. Sometimes they get too far ahead into unknown or difficult territory and your job is to bring them back into the reality of where you are within the overall process.

On the other hand, you may have to light an immediate fire under them in order to get them moving again. When they are slowed down, it's often a challenge trying to get them fired up again. They often take it personal that they have been slowed down and tend to feel stunted by you. Your encouragement goes a long way and when they know they have your complete support, they tend to develop an understanding along the way and will work at your pace. Balance is very important to the success of your footwork. Just as well as you are talking to your leaders, you should also be encouraging others to be good followers. When you are top heavy, the weight of upper influence will overpower or overshadow, lower influence and the followers will feel insignificant, unappreciated and disengaged when it should very well, involve both groups.

As you walk with your leaders, you must also walk with your followers and encourage them along the way. Your leaders will only be as effective as the gifts, skills and abilities of your followers. Without them, where is your tangible support going to come from? Leaders develop the plan and followers execute the plan. What's the sense in having a head, when there is no body? Likewise, what's the sense in having a body, when there is no head? They both are equally important and the balance of your leadership can and will determine the success rate of everyone achieving the goal.

The visionary should purge themselves of all the toxic energy, practices, behaviors and mannerisms that can ultimately, disrupt the flow of his or her entire operation and walk in a way that encourages and inspires others to follow suit. As you take steps toward success, they will too and as you succeed, they will too!

How can two walk together unless they are in agreement? Hold your head up and step in stride and in style, together!

CHAPTER SIX
Placing The Ball (*Tangible Responsibility*)
In The Gut of The Runner

The football is the tangible object, used within the game of football. You cannot play the game without this object. As a matter of fact, the game is identified by the object of the football. The football is an oblong object that can be thrown, kicked, pitched or handed off. You can score on three ways within this game and that is: the ball must cross the goal line in order to receive points, the ball can be kicked within the goal posts to score points or the defense can cause a safety, by stopping the offense within its own end zone. Even though the runner's body may be across the goal line, it's not considered a score until the ball actually crosses the white, goal line. The ball is the tangible object that must progress forward in order to achieve success. Without it, you gain no yardage and without it, you score no points.

Therefore, you absolutely get nowhere without the ball. It is the most important aspect of the game. You cannot use anything else in its place. It's the football or nothing. I don't care how big, strong, talented, skillful or ambitious you are, if you do not use the football during this game, you are just wasting your time.

> **Therefore, you absolutely get nowhere without the ball. It is the most important aspect of the game.**

The team bases all of its energy, fundamentals and skill sets around the football. Football is a team sport and it involves eleven active players on the field, at the same time, on the same team and its success is depended upon everyone fulfilling their individual assignments during any given play.

The quarterback's responsibility after he or she receives the ball is to either throw the ball to an open receiver or hand the ball off to the running back and allow him or her to run for positive yardage. *If the play is going to be successful, the quarterback must effectively place the ball within the gut of the running back and then quickly remove his hand out of the way as to not cause a fumble.*

The hand off must be clean, quick and precise. The ball is not placed at the running back's waist or chest, but in his or her gut. The gut is flexible and provides cushion for the exchange. By placing the ball in the gut, it allows the runner to get his or her forearms and hands completely around the ball so the runner can advance forward without losing his or her stride toward progress.

In this chapter we will discuss the correlation of the football, representing the tangible responsibility of the vision that is set forth by the ministry or organization. The tangible responsibility is directly given in an attempt to progress towards the vision. Without the complete, direct responsibility given, the vision is subject to not being fulfilled. As the ball is hiked within the hands of the quarterback, it is now within his or her hands and what they do with it next, will determine what the team does.

The vision is within the mind of the leader and the only way it can be manifested is if the leader transfers the vision from their mind into the heart or gut of the supporting cast.

> **The tangible responsibility is directly given in an attempt to progress towards the vision.**

No one person can fulfill a major accomplishment upon their own, without the help, support or resources of someone else. Leaders should be great communicators who are able to articulate the vision to their support system and effectively hand it off into the spirit of their team. According to scripture, the spirit of man is located within the bowels or gut of humanity. That's why you often hear people say: *I had a gut feeling.*

The spirit is invisible, but it is the place where we receive our supernatural energy from. When vision is released into the gut of others, it provides the vision as well as the energy to accomplish the vision. The vision begins to stir the imagination, emotions, intellect and inspiration of a person and motivates them to participating within a certain capacity, leading to a desired end.

Leaders must share their vision. Leaders should share their vision within the company of those who have the ability to do something about it. When the ear gates hear the vision and they eye gates envision the vision, it immediately enters the energy center or spirit of a person and if they hear it long enough and visualize it for themselves, chances are: you have gained another runner for your vision!

When placing the vision within the gut of your runner, you must do it with a sense of excitement, strategy, carefulness and belief. If you don't believe in the vision, how can you hand it off for someone else to believe? They will typically feed off of your faith and belief and become inspired to offer means of support for what you are trying to achieve.

Don't put the vision into their hands, without first putting in into their gut. If the vision is given too soon or with little clarity, it can cause your runner to fumble and lose hope or progress within the vision. Wait until they have received it completely and consistently within their gut, before giving them the go ahead to run with it. Just keep stirring it up within their spirit and allow it to simmer within them and wait for it to bubble over with proactive excitement and willingness to get going.

A few examples of how to put the vision into the gut of the runner.
1. After receiving the vision yourself, expose yourself to more learning and listening opportunities to become more acquainted and acclimated within what you feel you are called to do or accomplish.
2. Call a meeting with your runners (those who have skill sets) to provide practical resourcing to your vision.
3. With knowing what it is that you want to accomplish, have some brainstorming with, What if?

What if we were called to build a 24-hour prayer court? What could that possibly look like and what are some things we would need to make it beneficial? Whatever your what if is: you must spend countless hours learning about it and educating yourself regarding it.

    4. Based off of everyone's skill set, have them to brainstorm their creative thoughts surrounding their areas of expertise and allow them to bring suggestions back to the next vision meeting.

Continue to have series of vision meetings and continue to learn as a group and become more educated around the possible opportunity of fulfilling the vision. Once they are well acclimated to the opportunities and challenges, the next stage is to assign tasks that will get you moving into the direction of what your trying to do. I am by no means an expert on this envisioning thing, but I have had many experiences on this subject and have found the journey to be vast, long, and yet very rewarding!

> **Whatever you're what if; is: you must spend countless hours learning about it and educating yourself abroad regarding it.**

It's always good to have all types of communication or personality styles on your envisioning team.

I. **A calm and steady communicator** – this person tends to keep everyone together and in harmony, despite the challenges and opposition.

II. **An internalizing, thought provoking communicator** – this person can carefully think things through, consider many obstacles or opportunities that lie ahead and possibly keep you from making big mistakes. This person can also gage the temperament of the group and affected persons.

III. **A courageous and bold communicator** – this person will ask the tough questions and see the great potential in taking necessary risks.

IV. **A detailed, oriented communicator** – this person will cause you to cross every (*t*) and dot every (*i*) in order to prevent you from getting yourself in any legal or unethical trouble and cause you to be profitable or successful on the other end and help to develop systems and strategies.

All of these communicators are necessary for a successful, accomplishment and regardless of how each one can disturb, upset or challenge you as a leader, you must allow their communication style to help shape the canal of how you will maneuver and obtain your vision.

Remember, a running back knows very well how to run, and all you have to do is get the vision into their gut and their skill sets will take them the rest of the way. In some cases, a visionary is not a runner, but they cast or release vision. Give the runner room to run and don't get in their way when they are trying to bring your vision to life. They shouldn't tell you how to cast and you shouldn't tell them how to run.

When placing the ball within a runner's gut, there is a sudden impact. Sometimes it hurts and sometimes it doesn't, but the runner certainly feels it collide against the outer wall and inner core of their gut. Your runners should become impacted in one way or another by what you share and they should absolutely, feel it. If they are not positively impacted, it could develop over time or they may not be a runner for your vision and that's ok. Just find someone else who is.

CHAPTER SEVEN

Releasing Vision To The Runners

Knowing the Play (*Vision*)

As we shift gears from the quarterback to the running back during the second half of this book, we will focus our attention on the detailed characteristics, abilities and disciplines of the running back position. The running back is built to take hits and massive blows.

The typical characteristics and skills of a Running back are:

- Size (5'9", 215 pounds) or more
- Speed
- Versatility
- Power
- Explosiveness
- Ability to change directions
- Good Memory & Short Memory
- Patience

While there are so many more qualities that's necessary to function within this position, these main attributes are essential to making a running back successful and progressive.

<u>Size</u> – Proportionate dimensions or overall magnitude of a person. Height & weight evenly distributed for effectiveness.

Vision Runners – must have a well-balanced knowledge base and understanding, while working to fulfill the vision.

They make good sense of the overall goal in relation to the specific task that supports what your trying to do or achieve.

Speed –They possess acceleration, but they should also be quick and light on their feet and able to hit the holes as quick as possible in order to avoid being tackled at the line of scrimmage.

Vision Runners – don't drag their feet and prolong projects. They are very responsible and get things done in an appropriate time frame without having to be often reminded or primed to fulfill their duties.

Versatility – is the ability to adapt to various situations or circumstances.

Vision Runners – are not stuck when one door closes, but they adjust and figure out alternative ways in getting the job done. They typically, multi-task and know how to change directions or adjust, mid-stream and will not spend time sobbing over what happened or what did not happen.

Power – physical strength and might; abnormal to the typical capacity of the same size.

Vision Runners – should be able to take disappointments, setbacks, opposition and possess a mentality that can get over being told "no" or consequential failures.

Explosiveness – the act of being fearsome or ferocious when tested or challenged.

Vision Runners – should not be afraid to face obstacles, but have a greater intensity to overcome challenges, determinate and not easy to give up or give in, without a real fight.

Ability to change directions – a change of course, turnabout or reversal in the opposite direction.

Vision Runners – need to be able, at the drop of a hat to go from one aspect to another, without any hesitation. Nothing will hardly ever be simple, easy or straight forward. They know when to pick up momentum, slow down and diverge when necessary and as needed.

Good Memory / Short Memory – A mental capacity of retaining information, reviving facts or events. Also, having a short memory by not remembering past mistakes, to the point that they hinder current or future productivity.

Vision Runners – must be able to remember the vision and the specific details that is required to fulfill the daily duties of achieving the vision. They should be great note takers and able to recall the necessary information, without calling the visionary every five minutes asking for facts, details or previously given information.

Patience – the ability to accept delay, trouble or suffering while waiting on an avenue of opportunity, without getting bent out of shape or disgruntled, or too eager.

Vision Runners – must trust the groundwork that they have laid and not become impatient when things don't seem to line up with what they've expected, but allow the process to run its course to the end. The running back will not be effective if he or she does not know the play in which was called. The play call is directed toward a certain area or hole and if the running back turns and goes the opposite way or into a different hole, they may not fulfill their responsibility or go where there's no team support. There is a play book that the running back must study and everywhere he or she sees their position, they must see which direction or hole the play calls for. The running back must study the play book, to the point of remembrance. Each play will possess a certain signal or symbol to advise him or her on the actual play that's being ran.

Vision runners cannot effectively gain much progress toward the objective if they do not know what the vision is. Visions are specific, but are often altered, changed, tweaked or redirected. And if the runner does not initially know what the vision is, they will have no idea of the intentionality in the first place.

To know means: *to have, to understand and to learn within your mind, a clear and complete idea and a skill set to accomplish it.*

> **Vision runners cannot effectively gain much progress toward the objective if they do not know what the vision is.**

Vision runners must take the time, initiative and willingness to just listen intently to what the vision is all about and absorb every aspect of it as much as possible. When vision runners are unclear of the vision and begin to make decision's towards going forward, it can easily cause an unexpected collision between runners, receivers and supporters. Runners also have a certain level of vision and because of their skill set, they are often quick to respond, but you must slow them down and make sure they completely understand what the expectations are and the responsibilities that are before them.

They can unintentionally work against what you are trying to accomplish just based on the fact that they are not completely aware of what the vision consists of. Vision also entails timing. Many of the goals that will need to be achieved will need to be completed within a specific time or timely manner. If they misunderstand, drag their feet or do something totally different, they can cause you to miss some very important opportunities that are connected into the capacity of your vision and *"I'm sorry"* won't get back what you've lost. As a vision runner, you must ask lots and lots of questions. If you are unsure about anything or just needing more information or understanding, please ask questions and do not think that you are upsetting the visionary or challenging what they have said.

If you are going to do your part on behalf of the team, it's completely necessary for you to be as comfortable in knowledge as possible while proceeding. Unnecessary guesses can be detrimental to your team, so know for sure what you are supposed to do and what's expected out of you.

> **Many of the goals that will need to be achieved will need to be done within a specific time or timely manner.**

If you are uncomfortable, it will create too much hesitation and you will not be able to effectively articulate, respond or implement anything in regard to the vision.

Know what it is and know what your expectations are and know where it's designed to take you. Once you have been handed the vision or tangible responsibility, do more research into the various aspects of the vision or the responsibility that's required of you. Never just assume and take for granted that you know what needs to be done because things change and you must stay abreast to all of the changes that have taken place or potentially could happen.

Don't proceed forward unless and until you can personally explain what the vision is and what you are expected to do. Know it! Know it! Know it! Your spirit will begin to shape the vision within your inward eyesight and provide you with internal pictures of what it can look like. When you can truly say: *I see it*; that's when you know you are ready to go.

A runner really doesn't know the vision until a willingness evokes within them. If you are not provoked, you really don't know the vision. Keep exposing yourself to it until it lights a burning fire on the inside of you. Know what you have to do and do it with your whole heart; energetically, with effort and eagerness. You know you know it when you can defend it. When you can state the cause and effect of what you are doing, it sets a precedence of "why" you are doing it and the need for it to come to pass.

CHAPTER EIGHT
Understanding The Timing *(Position)*

Timing is everything. The world itself is regulated by time. Every movement, progression or regression is regulated by time and beats. Timing is extremely important in every aspect of life. It is the one thing no one has any control over because it is in the control of a supernatural force, far beyond our own capability. Therefore, it is extremely important to work alongside and in conjunction with time because it can very well pass you by.

When a quarterback prepares to hand the football off to the running back, it is a designed play, regulated by timing. Whether the quarterback is to take two or three steps backwards or to the left or right; the running back should be right there in order to receive the handoff. If the running back is too soon, it will throw the play out of timing because the quarterback will not be in position to hand him or her the ball. If the running back is too late, it will throw the play out of timing because it will give the defense time to get into the back field and disrupt the play. The quarterback has his or her cadence and the running back has its own cadence as well.

When both the quarterback and the running back are on the appropriate cadence, the play is run with perfect timing and the chances of being successful are far greater than if they were off beat or out of sync. Within the competition of a football game the appropriate timing can be distinguished based off of the defensive strategy of how fast the defensive lineman gets within the backfield of a team or how fast their linebackers plug the gaps and holes of the offensive line. Once their timing is determined, the offense then establishes their appropriate timing in order to defeat the timing of the defense. In other words, the offense studies the defense in order to know its timing cadence and then counteracts what the defense does, so that it overcomes it's attempt to stop them.

Though in the real world, it's not that cut and dry to determine timing, it's still important to know and understand the typical obstacles that often interfere with whatever play that you are trying to execute.

If you study and discover all of the things that you will need to specifically achieve your goal, you can also know and discover the various obstacles or hoops you must go through in order to reach your destination. With that being the case, if you proactively prepare for the obstacles and the typical challenges you must face, you can have the appropriate timing to overcome them by your proactive approach toward blocking the obstacle from hindering your success.

> **In other words, the offense studies the defense in order to know its timing cadence and then counteracts what the defense does, so that it overcomes its plan to stop them.**

Appropriate timing can be discovered by effective, proactive preparation. When you prepare for the worst, you are prepared to receive the best! Your knowledge about certain situations can either help or hinder you. If you have less knowledge about a thing, it can often hold you up because now you have to do some investigation and contemplation on what to do in response to the obstacle, but if you discover the obstacles early and prepare in the event that they will happen, you will be ready when and if it does. One of the definitions for timing is: *the selecting of the best time for doing or saying something in order to achieve the desired effect.*

Vision runners have a certain dynamic about them that enables them to be in the right place at the right time and to do what needs to be done at the right time and to observe, look for and obtain appropriate resources. It's almost as if they are predestined for those certain moments when they are needed the most. A running back develops a good sense of timing due to the fact that they run the same play over and over again henceforth, they develop a certain timing regarding a certain play and learn to master it, even down to the millisecond.

Though the real circumstantial world doesn't quite work the same way, a vision runner has typically been in situations where they have been before and even though the situation may differ, the principle may still be the same, therefore, they are ready and in place and awaiting to make the next necessary decision. One thing to consider is that you do not always have the appropriate runners you need within your organization starting out, however, God through divine means, will often send you a runner at the time you need them the most. They are experienced runners and know how to do the specific task that's required and they do not need a lot of micromanagement. When a vision runner is over managed or suffocated, they lose their creative ability to willfully function and they can begin to make excuse and justification on why they should opt out. You give them the direction, facts and potential challenges and then you get out of their way and let them advance your vision to the next stage of development and accomplishment. The question remains: are you in the right position to make the best decision?

Timing also predicates position. When you are in the best position to receive the next opportunity, it gives you an upper hand on the competition and buys you more time in the event an obstacle occurs. I once had a manager say to me: our competitor has the same machines, the same downstream equipment and the same kind of buying power, but what makes all the difference is people. The right runner within the right position will bring you the best results!

When a running back is in the right position to receive the handoff from the quarterback, his or her feet are in the right position, the head is up and looking forward and the hands are in the right position to receive the football into the gut.

> **When you are in the best position to receive the next opportunity, it gives you an upper hand on the competition and buys you more time in the event an obstacle occurs.**

They are not to look downward to see if the football is in their gut because they could take their eye off of the opposition that's coming and lose sight of the visual opportunity.

They are taught to learn and trust the quarterback and that he or she is going to put the ball in the right place at the right time.

It's the runner's job to feel the football into their gut and proceed forward toward success. Sometimes being in the right position, means being in the right attitude, mindset or fiscal position. Vision runners must trust that their visionary has made the right decisions and will effectively set them up to succeed and not fail. Visionary's typically make decisions based off of the whole of the situation and what they are requiring the runners to do is often in chronological order of some sort. Vision runners are typically looking at where they currently are and may make decisions that only considers now and not for tomorrow, the day after or the time to come, but the visionary typically has a thought process of progression.

When there is no trust between the visionary and the vision runners, it's going to be quite difficult to advance and proceed forward in success because the mistrust will second guess decision making and the clashing of the team will create inner conflict and stunt the progress of the vision. Vision runners must keep their minds into whatever it is that they are doing and even when faced with opposition, they must not look defeated and solemn, but should always be looking for opportunities to overcome their challenges and keep the progress moving toward the desired end. As a vision runner, you will always have close calls, but you strive to stay a step ahead.

Remember, you are on the front lines of challenge and there will often be times when it looks like the obstacles that hit you will knock you down and take you out of the opportunity, but

> **As a vision runner, you will always have close calls, but you strive to stay a step ahead.**

you must not be afraid of the potential setback, bad news, disappointment or brick wall. Close calls will happen, but guess what? In the same way you overcame the last situation will be the same way you'll overcome this situation. There is an old saying that I'm sure probably developed out of the area of sports and that is: the clock is ticking.

What that means is that time is running out and we need to make quicker and swifter progress before we run out of time. Long before you see the time clock, you'll get a feeling within your gut when you know time is of the essence. When you are at this point, it must be clearly understood that goal setting is very important. Vision runners should have small goals that they are setting as they go along. Big success is a direct result of small, consistent success. Small goals should be achievable goals, not decisions that are based off of long shots, but small successes that slowly, eat away at the magnitude of enormous opportunities.

If something is working don't hamper it because of impatience or sudden, anxious achievement. Chip away at your goals and when you look up from all the work that you've done, you'll find yourself much closer than you ever would have thought. Develop your plan and work your plan. I also had a manager once tell me: *the big bucks will pay for themselves; but watch the pennies.* What he meant was that it's the small things that really matter. When you do small things well, it automatically causes you to receive big things. Big things are long shots that often do not require much detail, but small things develop consistency and repeatability and provide you a systemic process to achieving your success. As I fore stated, timing is everything and when you are in sync, time will work in your favor. When you miss the appropriate time, you also may lose some very important opportunities that you may never ever get to see again and although other opportunities may come along, it still may not meet or match what passed you by. Think ahead! Take the time to acknowledge time, take the time to appreciate time, take the time to adjust to time and certainly take the time to benefit from time, but just know that time waits for no one and time is its own keeper of time and without time, there are no opportunities.

Being prepared for when time occurs is the best way to maximize the moments that transpire! When you are in the right position, you should be thinking about conquering the objective (getting in the end zone). You should have eyes that see the objective as well as eyes that see the opposition and the opposition has its eye on stopping you, but your passion to reach your goal should become the mental power to break the tackles of opposition and break the goal line to success.

Who wants it more? Do you want it more than the opposition wants you and are you focused enough, strong enough, fast enough, agile enough to get to the first down yard marker or cross the finish line?

CHAPTER NINE
Proper Placement of Hands to Receive The Ball *(Tangible Responsibility)*

Though many may view this principle as insignificant and irrelevant, this skill set plays a very important part within the receiving process of the ball from an effective stand point. The placement of the hands is strategically, positioned depending on which side the running back will receive the ball. If the running back is running to the left side of the quarterback, then his or her right hand should be located at the upper chest cavity and the left hand beneath the belly button. If the running back is running to the right side of the quarterback the left arm should be at the upper chest cavity, while the right arm beneath the belly button.

See images for details:

Left Hand Handoff   **Right Hand Handoff**

Once the ball is placed within the gut, the running back will retract their elbows downward to squeeze the ball between their arms for ball security and protection.

The running back must leave enough room between both arms in order for the quarterback to completely and successfully place the ball within his or her gut. When running backs do not have their hands in the proper position it could very well cause a fumble or prevent them from receiving the ball. Once the running back successfully receives the ball, the running back places his or her hand around the tip of the football in order to keep it tucked in. The hands are the key to keeping the ball safe and secure within the grip and gut of the runner as he or she progresses through the challenge of the defense. The defender's responsibility is to try and tackle the runner or strip the running back of the ball, so that they can recover it for themselves and take over responsibility of it.

Discipline is required from the runner to hold his or her hands within the right place; not too high and not too low. Timing to squeeze down on the ball is as important as receiving the ball. Therefore, discipline is required to hold your hands in a certain position and certain range of motion in order to have a flawless exchange between the quarterback and the running back. Practice makes perfect and the longer you do it together, the better and smoother the exchange will become.

When you are a vision runner there are small, tangible responsibilities that you must accomplish prior to the big stuff. Its sometimes doing the small, gritty, insignificant or dirty work that are oftentimes behind the scenes. For a running back to make a long yardage run is glamorous and often far, few and in between. However, they are mostly needed to make hard, long achieved yardage in order to progress the ball for more opportunities to score.

Gaining the tough yards is the most challenging work and you build a name for yourself by achieving short yardage plays. Running with vision, requires you to do the intangibles that seem small and irrelevant, but are very necessary to the overall goal or objective.

> When you are a vision runner there are small, tangible responsibilities that you must accomplish prior to the big stuff.

Get your hands dirty and commit yourself to the small things and detailed things that must be carried out on a regular or as needed basis.

Toughness is not determined by great opportunities, but by overcoming tiny, nagging issues that confront you face to face. As a vision runner you must position yourself close to the visionary in order to receive, understand, articulate and carryout the vision. Intimate listening settings are vitally important for a runner to effectively receive appropriate information to the implementation of the vision. A strong desire to see the vision come to pass is definitely needed as the passion for the vision is transferred from the visionary to the carrier of the vision. A runner is one who must possess certain character traits that are necessary to provoking the vision out of the visionary.

Some qualities are necessary, but not limited to:

#1 Dependability
The quality of being able to be trusted and relied upon.

A visionaire typically shares the general vision with the total group or overall players within the entity, but they specifically share the responsible details with those who show direct, interest and support to the implementation of the vision. They are usually the ones who have carried out other tasks, small or large that have benefited the organization up to this point. They are singled out because of their faithfulness and or success to previous tasks and have proven themselves worthy of more responsibility.

#2 Effective listening skills

The ability to actively understand verbiage, concepts, ideas and instruction by showing interest and asking questions that cause the speaker to go deeper in their explanation.

A visionary is looking for the ones who clearly see and understand the information and offer suggestions, relative toward the end result of the vision. They are not interested in those who waste time and derail vision, by asking intentional, improper questions. If one really does not understand, but truly seeks to know; that person will be viewed as one who really wants to support the vision.

#3 Initiative
A person who is self-disciplined and takes it upon themselves to fulfill tasks, aimed at accomplishing the vision without being poked or prodded to do so.

A person who shows much interest and tries as best they can to eliminate burdens by taking on a specific responsibility and understand they must make the work easier. Having someone look over their shoulder constantly, is a burden to them, so they get all the information they need to be successful, then galvanize his or her resources needed and implement them and bring back the report of their doings and or findings.

#4 Confidence

Assurance in ability of oneself to become capable or able to do whatever is necessary to carry out a task, function or responsibility.

A person who possesses confidence is a person with whom you can entrust responsibility. Their task will typically be performed at the highest level of their capability because their standards are much higher as a result of their experience or bar of expectation.

A vision runner should always be available to learn more about the vision and how significant their role will be within the whole scheme of things. Getting off to a great start is vitally important to the one who really cares about their potential success.

> **A person who possesses confidence is a person with whom you can entrust responsibility.**

Great running backs articulate just before the ball is hiked and placed within their gut, raise up on their tippy toes in order to get a great bounce and take off from their still position. They reinforce the principal of gaining greater momentum at the onset and getting off to the right start. Being in position is not just being available and right by the leaders' side, but it's all of the necessary preparation that one takes in order to gain the advantage or the upper hand.

CHAPTER TEN
Receiving The Ball *(Tangible Responsibility)* In The Gut

The running back understands that it is not their job to grab the ball or reach for the ball, but it's the quarterback's job to place the ball within their gut. As long as their hands and arms are in the right position, the handoff should be flawless! The timing is just as important as the placement of hands and arms from the running back and the precise turning of the quarterback and placement within the gut of the running back. If the running back reaches and tries to grab the ball, he or she can easily fumble through a mishandling or improper exchange between both players.

The smoother the exchange, the quicker the transition and potential success of the play! The running back must have a discipline in receiving the ball effectively from the quarterback, so that the running back can focus on the proper hole, immediate opponents and segment of success. The running back is not responsible for how the ball gets into their gut, but they are responsible for the health of their gut in order to receive the impact.

Vision carriers are not to force the hand, nor control the visionary's responsibility to share the vision, but they should position themselves and prepare to properly receive the vision. The impact of the exchange can be overwhelming; therefore, the vision carrier must develop a mindset of expectation. It is hard to perceive what the mind cannot conceive, so a vision carrier is responsible for developing their mind in order to be able to handle the magnitude of the vision and the amount of effort, energy and resources it's going to require for the vision to manifest.

> **The impact of the exchange can be overwhelming; therefore, the vision carrier must develop a mindset of expectation.**

Receiving the vision in the gut is more than just hearing about it, buts it's accepting a tangible responsibility that is necessary for its potential triumph.

What are you willing to do? It's not always about what you can't do or what you've never had to do, but it's about what you're willing to do as a result of your belief and commitment to the fulfillment of the vision.

When you are privileged to receive the vision, you should think about it, meditate upon it and envision it with your internal eye. You do the vision justice when you can take the time to play it out within your mind and discover your role within the plan. Once you have accepted it, you must develop passion towards it and allow yourself to become vulnerable to where it may possibly take you, as long as it's not illegal, unethical or inappropriate.

The quarterback or visionary must freely give the vision away and into the hearts and minds of its carriers. Those runners (vision carrier's) see it as an honor to be given a tangible responsibility. They major in carrying out specific tasks and welcome individual responsibility. They take ownership as a person of influence within the team and strive to get the job done. When the vision gets into their heart (gut) they become fully committed to the vision and dedicate their time, energy and efforts toward fulfilling their specific obligation.

They understand if they fail to do their job, they will lose credibility with the leader and supportive team and it can very well set back the entire goal. Can you be trusted to do your part and seeing it all the way through to the end?

Many health-conscious people take pride in showing you their six pack (gut). Its typically tight and narrow, but really tuff. They challenge you to punch it and watch how it doesn't cave in and the amount of pounding it can take. The stomach can take hard impact because of the shape it's in and so should it be with your heart. Your heart should be exercised in strong work ethic, determination, forgiveness, purpose, passion, healing and etc. When your heart is clear of negative debris and filled with possibility, it too will become strong and able to endure the impact of failure and the impact of vision.

The tangible responsibility that you are given as a vision carrier must be taken seriously. When you find out what your role is, you should seek to respond to these questions:
#1 Do I understand my defined role?

#2 What is my relationship to the responsibilities that are connected to that of my own?

#3 Do I need to develop a sub-committee or team to fulfill my obligation to the vision?

#4 What resources or networking connections do I have or need to make in order to complete my task?

#5 Have I considered the effectiveness of my task?

Like: efficiency, low-cost, systemic processes, quality, consistency and transitioning into the next task.

Your objective to completing your task should be, to get the job done no matter the obstacles, but to perform it with your complete focus and great attitude. Your attitude must develop a cohesion with that of your leader.

Even though things may not make much sense to you or you're not quite sure you should be doing what you were asked to do, you should not be hard to work with or bad mouthing your leader.

> **When your heart is clear of negative debris and filled with possibility, it too will become strong and able to endure the impact of failure and the impact of vision.**

Offer suggestions and be clear in your explanation, but don't work against your leader just because you have another perspective. How you articulate your perspective can determine whether or not it is received or not received by your leader. Just as the running back is not focused on, nor worried about the handoff, neither should the (vision runner) be focused on or worried about receiving the vision from the leader.

The focus should be: once you receive the vision, what are you going to do with it once it's in your heart. You must take the initiative to proactively build your personal skills so that at any given time, you can be ready to effectively carry out the tasks that are within your assignment. As backwards as this may sound, but as the vision runner focuses on his/her intangibles and perfect them to the best of their ability, it is what pulls the vision out of the visionary and forces shared responsibility toward its desired outcome. In other words, as you personally get better the vision becomes more exposed because it needs you in order to make it come to pass. Talent and skill provoke vision!

Talent, skill and wisdom draws the attention of vision and vision chooses the appropriate person to carry out its agenda. The better you become, the more you position yourself to be chosen by vision. Vision will then get into your mind and begin to direct your talent, skills and wisdom. Vision is not embodied by you, but you become embodied by vision and vision leads you to where it is destined to go. Vision can be accomplished much quicker and smoother depending upon those who have the abilities to carry it out.

Your personal devotion and investment into yourself will greatly improve the chances to fulfilling the goal. Half committed and half-hearted intentions will only prolong or derail an organization or person from the proper course of direction. When you take a very important responsibility and place it within the hands of a very capable person, great things can happen!

Whether it is a simple or not so simple task, the chances of completing it are far greater when the person assigned has a tremendous ability. What are you developing yourself to do well within?

> **Talent, skill and wisdom draws the attention of vision and vision chooses the appropriate person to carry out its agenda.**

What do you have to offer any organization who are looking for great success?

Even though the handoff may not always be perfect and the relating of the vision is not articulated with every minute detail, the very capable person can receive it and go above and beyond what may have been anticipated.

Having your hands in the proper position can mean:
- having the right attitude
- having a thought-provoking mindset
- having the right work ethic
- having the right determination
- and having the right plan of operation

When a portion of the vision is given into your hands, you are personally responsible for fulfilling your task and then preparing yourself to carry the next available task within your very capable hands.

Your hands should be trusted hands! Hands that can reassure the visionary and provide confidence to the team. This is your opportunity to prove to yourself and others that you are very capable of carrying a task all the way through to the end and doing it with dignity, style and class!

You must continue to speak to your hands! Encourage your hands! Manage your hands! Develop your hands and ultimately, clap your hands with celebration of achieving your goal!

CHAPTER ELEVEN
Running To The Right Hole
(When, Where and How to Proceed)

The running back should also have great vision. It is his or her job to first of all fulfill the designed play, but if the original hole is blocked, congested or just not available, it's his or her job to identify another open hole or gap to run through. Some of the greatest running backs possess the skill of patience. Patience waits for the blockers to confront their opposition and push them aside or tie them up until the hole opens up. In the mean-time the running back stalls time, hides behind their blockers and stays on his or her feet until the hole actually opens up and then they run through it. Most of the time, the running back should go through the hole that the play was designed to go through, but sometimes the right hole can be the wrong hole.

The holes are the gaps between the offensive linemen and the defensive linemen. The offensive linemen are given the task to create a gap for the running back to proceed through and depending on the defensive setup, speed of the defense and timing, the running back has the task of running through the intended gap. The offense knows where the gap should be, while the defense is unaware and trying to figure out where the running back will go.

> **Most of the time the running back should go through the hole the play was designed to go through, but sometimes the right hole can be the wrong hole.**

Running backs are often challenged with proceeding to the hole or gap too soon, before their linemen creates the actual gap. That's why it's so important to wait until the hole opens up before proceeding forward because you can easily get out in front of your help and lose progress or momentum in achieving your goal. It's a designed play, with a designed hole and your team knows exactly where that is. On the other hand, the defense has to guess or anticipate where they think you are going, but you have to beat them to the hole with quickness, power and agility.

If the designed hole is simply not available, then the running back must have vision to pursue another hole where he or she can run through to go forward. Having vision will allow you to see the challenge, utilize creativity, speed, agility and strength to either reverse directions, break tackles or juke a defensive player. Running backs are typically taught to hit the hole fast and hard. They understand that the window of opening may be very slim and sometimes what use to be a big opening, closes up really fast.

Too often, vision carriers allow their emotions and intellect to get in the way of what they are supposed to be doing, where they are supposed to be going and how they are supposed to do it. He or she must have tremendous discipline and not fight against themselves regarding what they think is best. Laziness sometimes plague a carrier because they reprioritize or minimize the value of ceasing the moments of opportunity. One of the greatest enemy phrases known to mankind is: 'I'll wait and do it tomorrow'.

In many cases tomorrow had never come and you cannot decide to wait until you get ready, but you must take full advantage of your right now moments of possibility.

Vision carriers can easily get ahead of the visionary and begin making decisions and doing things that are not in line with the vision. Just because a window of opportunity has closed, does not give the carrier the right to cease another opportunity. It may be that the carrier just has to wait and be patient for the timing of God. The vision carrier finds that out as they check with the visionary and receive new instructions. When you make a decision that has not been affirmed by the visionary, it could be because it is out of line and does not fit within the whole scheme of things within the long run. You could spend unnecessary time, money and resources that will cost you much more in the long run. As tempting as the opportunity may be, learn how to develop a patience and a commitment to touch base with the visionary and make sure that it's in line with the overall vision of the organization.

A vision carrier must learn to do the right thing. The right thing is not always determined by the carrier themselves, but that of the visionary. In the moment, you can very well think that making decisions is the right thing, but following specific directions is the right thing. If it is ultimately the wrong thing, you cannot be blamed for doing what you were asked or informed to do, unless you have been given an open-ended decision-making authority that gives you the flexibility to call your own shots, when necessary. If you're not sure, attempt to contact the visionary and get clearance to make the best decision. It doesn't take away from your ability or your competence when the wrong decision is made. Sometimes the wrong decision is just the wrong decision, but the blame will fall on the authority of the one who gave the permission to make the decision. Running through the right hole or doing the right thing, may entail not doing anything at all. Do not force yourself into having to make decisions that you are not ready to make, instead, pray and use your patience, wisdom and discernment. Ask yourself, is there a gain or a loss? Am I stuck with what I've made the decision on or is there any wiggle room with the result of this decision?

> **In the moment, you can very well think making a decision is the right thing, but following specific directions is the right thing.**

Typically, when the visionary gives a specific instruction they have already thought about the potential issues, opportunities and problems that could occur regarding any decision, therefore, it's the carrier's responsibility to just carry out the task without second guessing or questioning. The right hole constitutes the right thing and when you do the right thing within the moment of opportunity, it can yield a great amount of success. Many people have lost their job due to not following specific direction or orders and have cost organizations tremendous and unforeseen loss.

Don't allow yourself to get caught up in the moment of thinking you know what's best above and beyond that of the visionary, just do what you have been asked to do and as you develop trust with your visionary, you will also gain a greater opportunity to make wise decisions on your own.

The best coaches understand that while they are calling plays on offense, they must also call them with a defensive mindset. They see how the defense is lining up and playing against them and they call offensive plays based off of the approach of the defense. When they call a play, it is considering the defensive strategy of the opponent and it is then played like a chess match. Sometimes, depending on what position you play you are not aware of the specific strategies of your opponent. That's why in most cases it takes someone who can see the whole field to make the proper call.

They are paying attention to the timing, scheme and position of their opponent. They are coordinating conversation with other appropriate coaches and game-planning on how to be best successful. If they are not, they are not putting their team in the best possible position to win and actually end up beating themselves by not playing to the defensive weakness. Well, in the same way the visionary has to do his or her homework and discover the potential enemies of the vision.

Even though there are various moving parts within a vision, the visionary must think about the potential barriers and provide proper recourse to the carriers in the event they run into a brick wall or clogged opportunity. Rehearsing various strategies is what makes an organization great! As a matter of fact, the task and strategy you have been given should already encompass the opposition and even though it may not be smooth sailing, you can still have a confidence of maneuvering because of a well thought out plan.

The Running Plan should consist of:

#1 Strength – Aggressive, quickness to the point of attack, before the defense does

#2 Speed – Aggressive, quickness by the running back to the line of scrimmage, before the defense can act

#3 Skill – Plays and schemes that provide misdirection in order to confuse the defense

Runners for the vision should be non-procrastinators, who quickly embrace the opportunities set before them before the window of opportunity closes and do it in a way that mystifies an opposer, before they can react to what has happened.

Questions to consider:

1. Are there any potential legal issues regarding possibility?
2. Do we have the right resources in place to address them?
3. Is there someone on the other side of the opportunity in which we need to have discussion with?
4. Is the decision, task and or acquisition of a thing, moral and ethical?
5. Does it make sense to do it now and if so, why?
6. Do I have a way to sustain it once I receive it?

CHAPTER TWELVE
Having Vision To Make Necessary Adjustments

Running backs are a unique group of athletes. They work hard at developing certain skills and abilities that will give them the upper edge on their opponent. They try to become bigger, faster, leaner and stronger in order to break tackles and out run their competition. However, there is one thing that sets a runner apart from all the rest and that is the ability to adjust on the fly, while they are in pursuit of their goal.

When a planned play and direction of the hole has been determined, it is the runner's job to view or investigate the situation prior to him or her hitting the appropriate hole. Once the hole has been identified as closed or clogged, the runner must then look for another hole or direction to run in and make decisions to speed up, slow down, turn in or turn out, duck or leap. The key is to not run right into a wall of defense, knowing that you're not going to get anywhere.

The runner has to also develop a patience or hesitation, not towards the vision or goal, but patience regarding the window of opportunity. Waiting for the right opportunity to open up calls for a certain wisdom and the hesitation makes way for a clearer or less congested pathway to proceed through to a favorable result.

Well, the same holds true for the runner of the vision. He or she must know the responsibility or next step of the vision and investigate whether or not the task or goal is achievable and determine whether or not to keep moving forward or make a necessary adjustment.

> **The key is to not run right into a wall of defense, knowing that you're not going to get anywhere.**

Even though the visionary lays out the vision and disperses the responsibilities, things will tend to not go directly as planned.

Therefore, one must create opportunities by adjusting and redefining what it means to accomplish a certain thing. Keeping your eyes open and observing the playing field can ultimately lead to more progressive success. Analyzing the defense, kind of prepares you for the type of adjustment/s you must make. Also, scouting the defensive player helps you to know the type of defender he or she may be.

Adjustments can also be described as change. What type of changes need to be made in order to tweak how you arrive at your goal without, necessarily tweaking the vision or objective itself? Typically, what you are facing is not going to change. Its goal is to get in your way, slow you down and try its best to prevent you from achieving, but sometimes, you may have to change the way you do some things, midcourse and become flexible and unpredictable yourself.

Change does not always constitute the extremity of doing something totally the opposite of what you were doing, but it can be as simple as: changing direction, changing speed, changing the pace of momentum, changing your approach or changing your perception. These adjustments are typically the result of the changing dynamics that come with opposition. They force you to adjust, but when you stay stuck in a certain mode or way of doing things and do not give yourself permission to adjust, then you handicap yourself from overcoming the hurdles of change that present themselves anew and afresh.

I have discovered and have even learned to appreciate opposition because it serves as a growth mechanism for the opportunist. While challenges are intended to impede your progress, they are also designed to force toughness and creativity out of you. How are you going to overcome this challenge?

A few questions to consider when faced with a new challenge:

1. What is my goal or immediate objective?
2. What is within my means of ability?
3. Can my means alone, get me to my objective?
4. What am I missing that's needed to achieve?
5. Do I have access to what's missing or can I acquire it?
6. What opportunity will I lose, if I can't get what I need?
7. Is it worth me trying to figure it out or should I let this one pass me by?

While there are obviously more questions to consider, I believe these few questions will help you to determine your own motivational level to approaching your challenges and to help discover your immediate response to change.

Running backs who do not make necessary adjustments are considered as downhill or north and south runners. This just simply means that they are strong and most effective when they are only asked to run one way, but when facing various obstacles, they are limited in their ability to be elusive, so they just plow into the brick wall and typically that's where they stop. On the other hand, when you are flexible, elusive and quick to change, you have more opportunity to gain more yardage and the possibility of being more successful is available and most of all, fun!

Most professional teams have a down-hill runner and an elusive runner, but there are only a few select teams who have a runner who can perform both. It's not because teams don't pick a runner who can perform both, but it's because there are far, few and in between runners who are capable of doing both. Great runners are hard to come by, who possess all the skills, characteristics and attributes that can do it all.

> Most professional teams have a down-hill runner and an elusive runner, but there are only a few select teams who have a runner who can perform both.

Do you want to be a great runner or just a good runner?

The mentality of a runner knows what makes good, good and what makes great, great.

Therefore, the visionary and or organization must know the kinds of questions and skillsets to look for in someone who is good and someone who is also great.

The visionary is more comfortable and confident, when he or she can hand it off to someone who is great at what they do. A runner who is great will be completely accountable to and for the task. He or she will graciously accept the responsibility, see it from start to finish, incorporate their expertise within the task, figure out what adjustments need to be made, fully commit themselves to the task, determine and connect necessary resources that's needed and take full responsibility for its success and or failure. That's greatness at its best!

Visionaries or leaders do not take pleasure or pride in handing their very important task within the hands of failure and mediocrity. They want whatever they envision to be successful, therefore, they have a good idea on who's who. If you are not being asked or challenged to carry important tasks for the organization, chances are you are being looked over because of unknown, unproven or untrusted abilities. If that's the case, do not get mad or upset at the visionary, but work on your skills. Work on your knowledge. Work on your commitment and prepare yourself to carry out those things that are vital to enhancing your organization.

If you are being asked to perform such responsibility, it means that you have been approved and affirmed by leadership to handle such business and your level of confidence should peak, along with the weight of what's being asked of you. Do not allow over confidence to shortchange your work ethic and think that you can just slide through to victory regarding any task. Take it seriously.

Life is all about adjustments.

Adjustments that have to be made whether we are ready for them or not.

Your greatness will be defined by how well you overcame the

> **Do not allow over confidence to shortchange your work ethic and think that you can just slide through to victory for any task.**

odds and still found a way to be successful. Adaptation is really a skill in knowing when to turn the pressure up and when to turn the pressure down. It's actually gaging a situation and determining when, where and what to shift in order to escape the odds and pursue the goal.

Losing or failing can create a defeated atmosphere. One that is shaped by warp fundamentals that may have been ignored, unused or unappreciated. Losing is not the worst thing that can happen, but there is always a lesson to learn. What could you have done differently? What could you have done better? What changes could you have made to avoid failure or at the very least minimized it? Who could you have reached out to, to assist you with this project? What decision set you back, rather than propel you forward? These are just some of the questions that you can ask when failure shows up as your end result.

If losing is going to be worth it, lose with the assurance that you have given an honest and complete effort.

Winning isn't everything, but putting your best effort forward stabilizes the mind when losing is inevitable.

CHAPTER THIRTEEN
Running With Authority

Running with authority is what separates good running backs from great running backs. Great backs have great vision, hit the hole quickly, break tackles and turn on a burst of speed in the open field and are less likely to be caught from behind. Authority is a certain level of confidence that causes one to function far superior than another and it has no fear of opposition, but is relentless toward achieving its goal.

Great runners don't apologize for their tenacity and injury they may cause to the opposition, while focused on their goal. They blame the opposition for having the audacity to think they can stop them.

> **Authority is a certain level of confidence that causes one to function, far superior than another and it has no fear of opposition, but is relentless toward achieving a goal.**

They actually strike fear in their opponent's heart and make them think twice about getting in their way and trying to prevent them from scoring.

Great running backs actually punish the tackler, by hitting them first, before the tackler can get their arms around them. They keep their legs moving even if the tackler has their arms around any part of their body.

They don't easily give up and allow themselves to be stopped before reaching a certain amount of success and they keep their eyes on short and long-term goals, with no satisfaction unless or until they have achieved them.

Runners or supporters of the vision should possess the same kind of mentality when it comes to carrying out appropriate tasks. They should never regret moving forward and should proceed with a vigor and consistency that makes it hard for anyone to try to stop its progress. Every step should be well defined and sure that others feel a sense of being left behind, so that in order to catch up to them, they need to change their mind, strengthen their own ability and conform to a stronger mindset in order to participate or contend against its progress.

Effective vision carriers do not second guess themselves and lose momentum because of unknown doubts and or fears, but they clash head on with obstacles and obstructions that get in the way of where they are and where they are trying to go. The end result is too important to them and their focus is on what can and shall be, verses what may or may not be. Failure or non-achievement is not an option for them and their mental capacity is far stronger to reaching success because of their fixation on the prize.

When a vision supporter carry's the vision forward, he or she does not easily give up because of difficulties and setbacks, they press on through proactive, stimulation that doesn't often require outside influence. He or she is self-motivated and knows what to do in order to regain strength for the task and will persevere hard times, despite what's going on in his or her personal life, and refuse to allow it to come between what they are called and equipped to do concerning the vision. His or her authority is not limited only when things are going right, but its even implemented when things are not going so right. He or she does not focus on what cannot be controlled, but rather what is within his or her power.

Running with authority is established within the running back by the way he or she develops their psyche and physical body such as:

1. Wisdom
2. Determination
3. Awareness of success, goal markers
4. Leg strength
5. Agility

The vision runner must prep their mind and bodies to carry out the work, so that mental, emotional and spiritual fatigue will not slow them down or create a spirit of abandonment within them. Strengthening your legs is vitally important because it is symbolic of: committing yourself completely to the task. Without commitment, it will be extremely difficult to carry out what's necessary to accomplish the vision.

What organizations need are vision carriers who are committed and focused on fulfilling the goals and dreams of the organization.

> **His or her authority is not limited only when things are going right, but it's even implemented when things are not going so right.**

Everyone succeeds when the team is honed in on the goal or objective!

It is ultimately about acquisition. What is the team acquiring as it progresses along the way? Is it acquiring allies, networks, financial capital, land for growth and more skilled team members? Running with authority eventually separates itself from the rest! The burst comes as a result of open opportunities that the team has taken advantage of and acquires subsequently. The organization is in an overall, better position than its competitors and or industry it does business within.

Barriers or obstacles that seem to impair a vision runner may slow down the runner, but because of the commitment and relentless attitude he or she possess, it's almost next to impossible to hold him or her back. He or she keeps trying and trying until the opposition has been outsmarted, overpowered, outlasted and defeated. Scars and bruises from the collision only serve as motivators that fuel the passion and determination of the runner.

Even though vision is serious, complicated, difficult and rewarding, it is yet important that you strive with integrity, morality and ethics that do not devalue the game, the position you hold or the organization you represent. You should not be out to injure anyone else's career just for the sake of success. Life and the people who you compete against are human just like you. They bleed, hurt, tire just like you. They typically have families and people that love them as well and folks who are cheering in their corner too.

Respect yourself, your organization, the position or title you hold and the competition.

If you are going to succeed, do it without cheating or unjust interaction. Cheaters never win because when integrity is compromised, it cheapens the

> You should not be out to injure anyone else's career just for the sake of success.

accomplishment and never gains the full appreciation that is given to those who succeed.

Authority does not warrant disrespect, but because of its nature, it recognizes the dignity of the other and does not take for granted that it can be on the side of no authority at any given time. Success requires a level of tenacity, but its focus is not so much on damaging the opponent, but more so on achieving its goal. Running with authority hinges on the toughness of the runner, who is able to borough through the attempted, barricades of the opposition. Toughness can handle the pressure, proposed and still be successful!

Have you ever witnessed success that never came with some level of opposition? That's why you must take authority and declare your psychological, superiority over that in which tries to prevent you from achieving. It's a mind-set. You are what you think about yourself and only you can talk yourself down to a place of inferiority. Don't allow the pressures and circumstances of adversity to dictate if you can win or not. Instead, activate confidence, square your shoulders, hold your head up and fix your eyes on the prize.

Authority must be the very first object of your attainment, without it, you are subject to losing, but with it, who can stop you? Once you acquire the authority, your opponent is at your mercy and must be in a mode of reaction or defense. The goal of a team is to keep the defense on their heels for long periods of time in order to wear them down and break their spirit of competition against you.

When you can effectively answer these questions, and step up to their demands, it's going to be next to impossible to stop you.

#1. Am I mentally, physically, emotionally and spiritually strong enough to believe I can achieve my goal?

#2. Do I possess or have a certain skill or ability that sets me apart from the rest?

#3. Does my psychological, stamina of tolerance exceed my desires of giving up?

#4. Have I learned how to keep one eye on the goal and the other eye on the obstacle and simultaneously, achieve as well as defend?

#5. Do I have a desire and ability to encourage myself and others along the way of achievement, regardless of the opposition? You now can run with **Authority!**

CHAPTER FOURTEEN
Gaining Yardage (*Momentum*)

The rule of thumb for great running backs is to touch the ball at least twenty times per game. That's a lot of work and wear and tear on the body. The objective of giving the great running back so many touches is because when given the ball, he or she does something special with it. The coaching staff and team trust him or her when the ball is in their hands. They just have a way of turning negative yards into positive yardage. Their unique and distinctive style carries the bulk of the offensive load and their number is called when the goal is within reach and winning is on the line.

It's a lot to ask for from one person, but time and time again he or she has proven them self and have gained the trust of the organization. The offensive plan is to pound the ball down the

> **The objective of giving the running back so many touches is because when given the ball, he or she does something special with it.**

other team's throat and wear them down, especially within the last minutes of the game. Are you built to last? Can your body handle the wear and tear of the tenure of the game?

Its great if you think you can handle the work load, but great running backs also have a wisdom that controls their skill. That is the wisdom to know when the play is over, take less punishment or run out of bounds and live for another play. Twenty yard runs and ten-yard runs are great, but so are three and four-yard gains. In the game of football, you have essentially four downs to gain ten yards and many times you can't get it all at once. Wisdom sometimes forces you to take what you can get and try to set up the next play or next opportunity to achieve the goal. The key is to gain positive yards and obtain the momentum in order to get the defense on their heels.

When you have proven yourself as one who can effectively carry out vision for an organization, you more than likely will play significant roles and be called on consistently. You just have a way of making things happen. You go above and beyond what your asked to do and you add a certain touch to it that often blows the mind of the visionary and team. Every task that you are given, you come through and it's just the small things or assignments that repeatedly get done.

As I stated earlier, I use to have an Operations Manager that once said to a group of leaders: "the big bucks will pay for themselves, but you have to watch the pennies"! It was then, I learned that small details fill the silo's of great plans. As a matter of fact, great plans come to fruition as a result of small details. So often we have these great ideas and massive visions, dreams or goals and we began to launch or start as if we are already there and that is a big mistake. Think big, but work smart! Don't make big decisions that could impact your progress, which wipes out everything you've worked so hard to accomplish. Minimize your losses, so that you can still survive the impact. Wisdom does not cause you to lose it all, but it is satisfied at progress and small increments of success, as you proceed down the road of possibility.

It is important for you to gain the momentum. Momentum is when things are going your way and you seem to have the advantage. The pendulum has swung in your direction and the energy level of your team is through the roof. When you have momentum working in your favor, you can rip the heart out of your opponent or obstacle and make them quit, stumble or get out of your way. All you need is small, consistent successes that continues to agitate your opponent and disrupt the confidence or strength of its existence.

Don't hurt yourself or your organization trying to do too much, too soon, without wise thought. Take a breather and regain strength for the next opportunity. As the old saying goes; Rome wasn't built in a day. Winning is winning, as long as you are winning! Whether its big win or little win, a win is a win! Great running backs know, as long as they make positive yardage, the chances of them getting the ball again are great. They know that positive yardage gets them closer to the goal and it potentially, sets them up for something bigger. Home runs are great, but so are base hits. In baseball, the goal is to get on base. If you get on base, someone else can get you home.

In football, all you need is ten yards at a time. There are many ways to get to ten.

> **Winning is winning, as long as you are winning! Whether its big win or little win, a win is a win!**

Such as: 2+8=10; 3+7=10; 4+6=10; 5+5=10; 3+4+3=10. You get the picture?

How many ways can I approach a situation and yield some level of success?

Approaches to accomplishing a goal by taking it one step at a time can be achieved within this fashion:

Short Term Goal – to increase first down productivity from 3 yards to 6 yards.

Observational questions:

Can I increase the amount of blocking time against the defender by one second to increase yardage?

Do I need to insert more misdirection plays that confuse the defense?

Do I need to draw up more plays, where the runner hits the hole quicker?

Does the runner need to develop more patience before hitting the hole?

Do I need to throw instead of run on first downs?

If I ask and respond to these various approaches, I have a better chance at gaining the extra yards, I'm looking for. Otherwise, If I keep doing what I've been doing, my yardage does not increase and I do not reach the short-term goal of productivity.

Approaches will vary depending on the type of position, skill or industry you are in. However, I must figure out the best questions to ask and respond to in order for me to be successful. Know your industry, know your job and understand how it works, so that you can ask the proper questions and provide the necessary responses of opportunity to effectively gain the momentum.

Momentum can be achieved by one play, one act or anything positive. Momentum is circumstantial. Anything can cause the momentum to swing, however, it can also be achieved by a sudden change in mentality and or emotion. When you decide to perk up, wise up, feel up and get up, you can swing the momentum your way. It's simple. Its forcing yourself to gain emotion around what you are doing and work harder at what you are trying to achieve.

When you can do something spectacular with your responsibility, you can shift the momentum and inspire and motivate your team! Why can't you be the one to shift the momentum? You've been watching everyone else do it from time to time and now it's your time! Do something great to gain the momentum.

In football, it's just called: *"making a play"*. Whether it's making a tackle, making an interception, throwing a pass, making a block, recovering a fumble, making a run or making a catch. Do something specific to either stop the progress of your opponent or something great to get you closer to the end zone. Momentum can happen on defense as well as offence, so both sides of the coin are applicable. Whenever you see an opportunity, go for it!

> **When you can do something spectacular with your responsibility, you can shift the momentum and inspire and motivate your team!**

A runner or supporter of the vision should always look for opportunities to achieve momentum in reaching the vision. Networking, connecting the dots and building relational bridges are what helps to gain momentum.

Every person has a special and unique resource that can assist you in accomplishing your goals. The bigger and stronger your network, the better it will be to being successful. Knowing and understanding your goal helps you to know who and what resources are needed. Therefore, meeting with the right people and solidifying the right resource will help you to gain momentum on a consistent basis.

Achieving small detailed tasks are essential for gaining momentum. Laser focus on fulfilling tasks that are in line with the vision are what motivates momentum as well. You cannot be confused on your next step or divided within your mind concerning what needs to be done. Good decision making is crucial to gaining a certain amount of momentum and making wise choices are very important to maintaining the momentum.

A vision runner does not waste a lot of time in between tasks. He or she consistently function in order to stay on top of responsibilities and never lose sight of what is to be accomplished. Every time something is achieved, he or she gets excited all over again because the finish line is getting closer and closer. There is no satisfaction because of one or two accomplishments, but complete satisfaction is not valid until the end goal is reached.

Vision runners understand the significance of their role and do not have to be talked up in order to get going. They don't need constant pats on the back in order to get motivated. They motivate themselves by completing their tasks and keeping a close eye on where they are verses where the goal of success lies, as the distance between their current progress to that of the whole, shortens, when their excitement builds.

Every line represents short progress. Momentum is continuing to go forward, regardless of opposition until you reach the next goal. Increase your will to gain momentum!

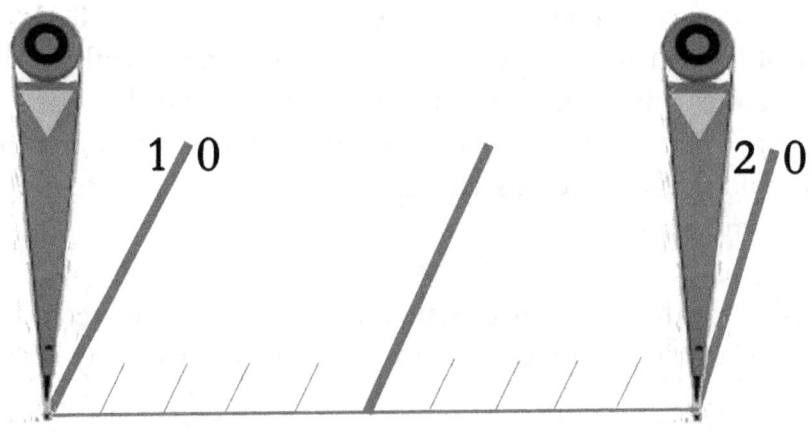

CHAPTER FIFTEEN

Scoring A Touchdown (*Accomplishing The Vision*)

A touchdown is worth six points. It is the highest scoring achievement within the game. You can earn one point by kicking the extra point, following a touchdown, two points by getting into the end zone following a touchdown, three points by making a field goal or you can score two points via a safety. Football teams play the game to score touchdowns, not field goals. Many games are decided by few points, so every point is important, but the ultimate objective is to score a touchdown.

Scoring a touchdown gives you points of success that hopefully places you ahead of your opponent. One of the most often stated slogans is: The greatest defense is offense! Whether it's one big play or a series of plays, scoring is what's most important. Running into the end zone is what constitutes a touchdown, not getting close to the goal line or right up to it, but actually crossing the goal line is what constitutes a score.

Scoring a touchdown doesn't always come easy, but it is also a reminder of the commitment, wisdom, grit, stamina, skill, fortitude and opposition that it took for you to reach your goal. They are attainable, but not without a lot of work. It comes with pain, fatigue, blood, sweat and tears, but it's worth it when you can achieve your goal and raise your hands in victory!

Winners write off the pain by being successful!

It is absolutely, always appropriate after scoring a touchdown for the coaches and staff to review tape, photos and scheme's to see how they scored. You scored, so what are you looking back for? They are looking to see:

What was the defensive scheme and set up?

What play was run, prior to the scoring play that caused the defense to scheme that way?

Who or what was the weakest link during the scoring drive?

> **Winners write off the pain by being successful!**

Those are just a few reasons as to why the staff needs to review how they scored. This approach helps to develop consistent strategy in order to continue scoring. It is a chess match all game long and those who play it best will usually come out on top.

Just as the runner scores a touchdown, so must a vision runner. Achieving success at what you set out to do is very important. While success is not necessarily measured by points, it is also measured by accomplishments. What you accomplish adds tremendous value to you and your organization. Initially, all accomplishments are worth it, but you must move to relevance, importance and influential success that truly make a difference, not just inside your organization, but to those who are outside of your company. When your success can positively impact those outside you, you stand the chance of growing your organization.

What does your organization offer or provide that fulfills the need of a consumer base? What do you do well that draws attention to your organization? This is why you've worked so hard at fulfilling your responsibilities, so you can build or create a market for your goods or services. Otherwise, why are you in business or working within a certain industry? You are there to make a difference and you are there to set yourself apart from the rest of those who may be servicing the same market or context you are serving.

Discuss what it is that you are trying to accomplish and then develop strategies and implement tasks that are in line with what it is you are trying to achieve. Keep your eye on the goal and do not let anything distract or deter you from reaching your goal. Yes, you get tired, but too much sleep is for those who are lazy and have no vision or goal to reach. Develop an attitude of second wind and keep striving until you get there. I know people often hurt you in the midst of striving for success, but don't give them too much power by allowing them to discourage you in the process.

After considering your goal, you must identify sequential steps that's necessary for accomplishing the goal. Once you have identified everything that needs to be done, begin assigning tasks and persons responsible to fulfill those tasks and everyone needs to be working on them simultaneously. That way when you come together, some things can already be done and checked off the list, instead of waiting for one task to be accomplished at a time. You can stay on task when your team is completing their assignments and progressing forward as you attempt to gain momentum and become successful. I will share with you a task completion format that I developed some years ago, called the "**Spider Walk Plan**". If you follow this format, it can help you to know where you start and how you finish. Most people have difficulty in knowing where and how to start and it tends to be the most frustrating thing when trying to accomplish goals, visions or dreams. Here are the various parts.

1) What is the goal, vision, job, task, career or title?

_____

2) When & Where is the date you'd like to achieve this?
When _____ Where _____

3) What are the boundaries of focus?
Purpose of goal (why?) _____
_____
Objective of goal (intention) _____
_____

4) Who and what are your (8) leg Support System?
1
2
3
4
5
6
7
8

5) What (4) leg Support System assist your Purpose?

1

2

3

4

6) What (4) leg Support System assist your Objective?

1

2

3

4

7) Assign specific duties for each leg within your Support System to fulfill the Purpose and Objective

Leg 1	Leg 2	Leg 3
Leg 4	Name, Date and Location of Vision	Leg 5
Leg 6	Leg 7	Leg 8

See diagram on next page

Purpose of Goal ━━━▶ (my why?)

Goal Completion Date & Location

⬇

```
Completion Date – **January 2025**

Location – **New Vision Christian Church**
           **9101 Blue Ridge Blvd., KCMO 64138**
```

Objective of Goal ━━━▶ (my intention)

Your Purpose and Objective are boundary lines that will keep you focused within the area of your operation. Whatever you may find yourself doing, you can always measure it up to your purpose and objective. **If it doesn't fit those criteria, then you probably shouldn't do it.**

To meet the spiritual needs of our communities within the Greater Kansas City area

To be a consistent resource ministry for our city

This becomes your plan of implementation that entails your goal, when and where you'd like to accomplish it and your support system, as well as defined responsibilities for each leg of support. **Walk out your vision effectively to the date and place of your ultimate desire!**

CHAPTER SIXTEEN
Celebrating The Victory!

Scoring a touchdown is a big deal. Never let anyone tell you that scoring is not that important and not worthy of celebration. I don't care if your team is actually losing and losing by twenty points; every person who scores celebrates like it's the very first score. Celebrating provides inspiration and provokes motivation. Players have even worked extremely hard on celebration dances, props and customs that reinforce their need to keep scoring. The crowd cheers and makes much noise, so much that the ground shakes and the energy in the building or space is electrifying.

To score and not celebrate is to not appreciate everything it took to get into the end zone and it encourages your supporters to stop cheering

> **Scoring a touchdown is a big deal.**

because it insinuates you really don't care. If you don't plan on scoring, you don't plan on winning and if you don't plan on winning, then why suit up for the game? Don't get involved with the team if you don't plan on being successful.

Some players go overboard and actually cross the line to what is ethically and morally appropriate to that which diminishes the art of scoring. Nonetheless, the score deserves celebration. Don't take away from what you've accomplished by doing something distasteful or inappropriate. Celebrate with dignity and remind your opposition that you're not finished scoring and that you operate with class and high aspiration.

Teams who do not celebrate a score, have no real enthusiasm towards winning, but those who do, change the atmosphere with excitement. When you can celebrate the touchdown, you can celebrate the win. Winning requires celebration! Let's define a win. A win within the confines of your overall objective does not necessarily, require a celebration. Some things are just expected and not too hard to achieve. However, when you have accomplished all of the necessary things to acquire a win; that's when you celebrate. You don't celebrate a two yard or five-yard gain, but you do celebrate a first down (ten yards). Ten yards earn you a new set of four downs, but your goal is to score a touchdown. And when you can actually win the game that's when you perform an all-out celebration.

You must also look at the cause for the celebration. It's one thing to be ahead from the beginning and blow out your opponent from the jump, but it's another when you've had to come from behind, create turnovers and make spectacular plays down the stretch. Coming from behind, as a result of tremendous odds to get a win is truly worthy of radical celebration.

The same holds true concerning organizations who yield a certain level of accomplishing success. They should learn to celebrate as a team and reinforce togetherness and hard work for overcoming whatever obstacles that stood in their way. When an organization or team creates a victory, they need to get into the habit of pausing from the efforts of tasks and celebrating the accomplishments that many have put into it toward victory. This shows appreciation and reveals to the team players how they are valued and worthy of recognition. It doesn't cost much to show forth a little thanks.

Celebrating a victory against all odds is what sends sparks of hope and inspiration throughout your organizational team. People who have utilized their skills just to make success more attainable have done so for the sake of the organization. They have sacrificed time, family and other opportunities because they are fully vested in the organization and a small investment of celebration is truly worth it. There is no blue print on how you can celebrate, but sometimes being creative in your celebration can stimulate more enthusiasm and creativity within the minds and heart of your team.

They want to do even more and areas and places where they may have been challenged, have now warranted various ways and methods of resolve, simply because they are now motivated to think a little more concerning their obstacles. Celebrating often says: let's do this again! When a team wins it provokes a desire to win again and again and again! Participating on a winning team is what draws other winners to your team. If you have a losing team, I guarantee it will draw other losers toward you. Winners like to hang out with winners and losers like to hang out with losers because the bar is not set too high.

> **It doesn't cost much to show forth a little thanks.**

Winning raises the bar of your individual efforts and gets into the habit of celebrating. Not many celebrate the trial of losing, but everyone loves celebrating the joy of winning.

Sometimes many organizations lose motivation because they are too lazy to muster up enough strength to celebrate a victory. They are too fatigued, busy or overwhelmed to take time out to celebrate. This is the worst attitude you can have because you devalue your support system and show them that it's not really a big deal to honor them for their success. Success is in a league of its own and not everyone can experience it on a small level, let alone a great level.

Honoring success, simply means that you respect it and that it required a lot of energy and effort to get within its presence and the reward of being in its presence is worthy of recognition. It's very difficult to be successful if you don't recognize it when it shows up. Taking success for granted insinuates that you don't need it and can live without it. I don't know about you, but if life never offered or yielded success, I don't think none of us would be here. So now that you have found success, celebrate it, honor it, respect it, surrender to it and build the moral of your team around it! Make success recognize and surrender to you because of your repeated effort to achieve it.

I don't want to send the message that the only time to celebrate is when you win. I think you should recognize and understand your wins, even though it may not be ultimate success. Sometimes your win could just be solidifying a few contracts, changing the moral of your team, decreasing your debt and increasing your bottom line. Your win can simply be because your team has given a greater effort than they had before, but fail to accomplish the overall goal. What I am saying is that a win deserves a celebration if it has any level of transformative aspects within your organization. You don't celebrate the loss, but you do celebrate the progress and you are better for it because you have improved who and what you are as a team. Everyone who has had anything to do with the success should be celebrated. Whether they served a minor role or played a major role. Small successes lead to Big success! No one is irrelevant within your organization from the least to the greatest. There is no insignificant role or role player.

Regardless as to how a person has impacted the team, all are worthy to be recognized, appreciated and celebrated. You must stop and ask yourself, if you take away what the least person has done, the question you must ask yourself is: could our success have been achieved without the influence or task of the least person? It takes all moving parts to make a whole and sometimes those people who do not shine in the limelight or stand on center stage get overlooked, while the outspoken and recognizable people get honored and celebrated. That's not fair to those consistent, behind the scene team players, who do their part day in and day out for the sake of the team.

In your celebrations, don't forget the small person.

CHAPTER SEVENTEEN
Putting Your Victory In The Past

Just a bit of a warning to you, do not spend too much time celebrating the same level or measure of success. Challenge yourself by going to another level or aspect of success. Do not just settle and have nothing more to work towards. A football team's ultimate goal is to win the championship. The highest level of success within football is reaching the Super Bowl. The Super Bowl consist of one, big game; actually, the last one of the season. It is what every team has worked so hard for to reach.

Each year, every team has to start over, typically with new and or different players to accomplish winning the ultimate prize. So, you play to win the Super Bowl, but even if you win two years in a row, you must forget about the last one in order to focus on the current one. Many people will constantly remind players of their accomplishment of winning the Super Bowl and repeat a mini celebration per every fan, but the player must psychologically forget about the last win and focus on the new season.

The evolution of time is a constant reminder that you must move on and not remain in the fog of the past. It's not that your victory is not worthy of remembering, but when you stare at yesterday, you miss the moment of today and have no awareness of what to do tomorrow. It doesn't mean you have to trick your psyche or lie to yourself about winning,

> **Do not just settle and have nothing more to work towards.**

but it does mean, you need not allow yourself to be satisfied with what has already been achieved. You must make a mental note that you've accomplished your mission and now there is a new mission you must embrace. Putting your victory in the past does not mean to forget, but to actually remember. Remember what you did to gain the success and put in the past the reward you acquired when you were successful because there is a new reward awaiting your arrival. Whenever training camp starts, should be the repositioning of the old success. That's right, old success. You can get comfortable talking about what you use to do and what you did last week, last month or even last year.

The truth remains, you must be prepared for a new season, new teammates, new leadership staff, new challenges and new opportunities. It is an attitude of a winner to not settle for meager, minor or temporary success, but consistent success. Dwelling on past success provides a bragging right for those to whom you competed against, but it does nothing for the present competition that is standing right in front of you or waiting to compete against you.

As the winning Super Bowl team forget about its past success, so must the team players within an organization forget about its prior success.

Organizations suffer when they embody outdated ideology, antiquated systems and old ways of communication that use to work in ages before.

> **You must make a mental note that you've accomplished your mission and now there is a new mission you must embrace.**

Supporters of a vision recognize that vision is for a specific time, specific reason and more than likely a specific context.

They realize they must make a mental shift and adjust to the new nuances that require new means and rules of engagement. The question is: how can I train myself to forget about past success?

1. **Decide what specifically you would like to forget, concerning a particular success.**

    - If there was a tangible reward given to you for your achievement, place it somewhere where you do not have to see it on a consistent basis
    - If it is an organizational award located in a particular place within the offices or campus, try to ignore looking at it as you pass by
    - Envision a newer version of it within your mind that has your name on it, so when and if you see the past one, it will look nothing like the new one you are working toward

2. **Even though you played a part of the last success, think about what you didn't accomplish, personally.**

    - Make a habit of repeating to yourself, audibly what it is you want to accomplish this time around

3. **Create your "*Spider Walk Plan*" and look at it on a daily basis as to infuse yourself with your current, goal objectives.**

    - Work some aspect/s of your plan on a daily basis

within the storage place of your mind, where you have stored the success. Putting it in the past helps to provide room for replacement of the new endeavor. Try to only remember your specific contribution because it may cause you to repeat the same kinds of behavior and effort that it took to be successful and you will need some of those memories as you go forward. Putting it in the past says, I did it, I achieved it and I want to do it again! However, you must have a short memory and not give it a long-term mantle within your mind. It must be removed for the next one to have its time to shine.

All of your achievements are being calculated within what is known as your legacy. As long as you are alive, you are building your legacy, but don't let your legacy be remembered for one moment of success, but many moments of success. People and society may forget about you, but they will always remember your legacy because your legacy lives on even in your absence. As long as your legacy can be remembered and living, your name will often come up as a result of your legacy.

This book is my third writing publication and when I was asked about the first book, I had placed it within the back of my mind, to where I really didn't focus on remembering I had written it. I knew I had written two books, but it didn't stand in my way in writing the second one and now the second one does not stand in the way of writing my third. I didn't forget it completely, but I did store it out of the way of my future goal. As it relates to legacy, you want people to approach and respect you not for a specific work, task or accomplishment you achieved, but you want them to approach and respect you for who you are and the tremendous contributions you have made in your life and society.

> **All of your achievements are being calculated within what is known as your legacy.**

They will know you are just a person to be well respected and acknowledged for the value of your worth and not because of a small contribution you made once upon a time.

So, what happened in the past?

From this point going forward, what is your next goal?

Blank Page

OTHER BOOKS BY DR. KEVIN L. HARRIS SR.

Where Do I Start? (How To Prepare A Sermon) ($21.99 + shipping)

Publisher: Trafford Publishing

The Necessary Journey: What God Uses to Push YOU into Your Destiny Paperback – January 26, 2015 ($16.99 + shipping)

This book is a 14-step process of Jesus' journey to the cross as He went through 14 stages up until His death. In each stage Jesus shows us: What He had to go through. Who His opposition was. The practical example and the Spiritual significance. In this book it will show us how to reach our destiny by following Jesus' example through hardship, agony and pain. But the end result is Resurrection or Destiny!

Publisher: Dr. Kevin L. Harris Sr.

Several books are in the process of being written by Dr. Harris and his next book is schedule to be released in 2020.

To purchase any of these books, please contact us via email at:
getjesussoon@aol.com

www.ingramcontent.com/pod-product-compliance
Lightning Source LLC
Chambersburg PA
CBHW050558300426
44112CB00013B/1975